Overthinking - The Silent Saboteur

Practical Techniques to Silence Your Inner Critic's Mind Chatter, Break Out of Analysis Paralysis, and End Self-Sabotage

Delia Sikes

Neel Mountain Publishing

Copyright © 2024 by Delia Sikes.

All rights reserved.

No portion of this book may be reproduced in any form without written permission from the publisher or author, except as permitted by U.S. copyright law.

Legal Notice:

This book is only for personal use. No one can amend, distribute, sell, use, quote or paraphrase any part of the content within this book without the consent of the author or publisher.

Disclaimer Notice:

Under no circumstances will any blame or legal responsibility be held against the publisher, or author, for any damages, reparation, or monetary losses, direct or indirect, due to the information contained within this book, including but not limited to errors, omissions, or inaccuracies. You are responsible for your own choices, actions, and results.

Please note the information contained within this document is for educational and entertainment purposes only. All effort has been expended to present accurate, up-to-date, complete and reliable information. No warranties of any kind are declared or implied. Readers acknowledge that the author is not engaging in the rendering of legal, financial, medical or professional advice. The content within this book has been derived from various sources. Please consult a licensed professional before attempting any techniques outlined in this book.

Contents

Introduction	1
1. What Is Overthinking and Its Impact?	4
2. Identify Your Overthinking Patterns	18
3. Break Free from Analysis Paralysis	44
4. Silence Mind Chatter with Practical Techniques	64
5. Enhance Self-Confidence with Self-Compassion	89
* Help Us Silence the Saboteur *	104
6. Reduce Nighttime Overthinking and Improve Sleep	107
7. Overcome Professional Self-Sabotage	121
8. Strengthen Personal Relationships	138
9. Holistic Approaches to Manage Overthinking	152
10. Commit to Long-Term Change	165
Conclusion	185
References	188

Introduction

I remember the day I sat at my desk, staring at an email announcing yet another promotion. This time, it was for someone less qualified than me. Someone who hadn't put in the years, the late nights, or the extra effort. My heart sank, and I felt that familiar tightness in my chest. "Why not me?" I thought. The answer was simple: overthinking. It had become my silent saboteur.

For years, I convinced myself I couldn't manage people. "What if I fail?" "What if they don't like me?" "What if I accidentally offend them?" "What if I make the wrong decisions?" These thoughts looped in my mind until I believed them. So, I never even applied. I watched others climb the ladder while I stayed put, shackled by my doubts.

Overthinking isn't just a minor inconvenience. It's a heavy burden that can crush your dreams and aspirations. I felt the emotional and psychological toll deeply. The frustration of seeing others move ahead while I stayed stuck was unbearable. It led to sleepless nights, chronic stress, and a constant feeling of inadequacy.

Battling overthinking and self-sabotage held me back from my career potential until I decided to change. I learned and internalized concepts that helped me break free from my self-limiting beliefs, and the results were profound. I combined my teaching skills and empathy into team leadership, transforming my career. I want to share what I learned with you because you can experience the same transformation.

So, what is overthinking?

DEFINITION: Overthinking is that relentless mental chatter that makes you question every decision, doubt every action, and fear every outcome.

It's the voice in your head.

- Perhaps it says you're not good, smart, or brave enough.

- Perhaps it says you could do the work, but you're no good at convincing others to support you.

- Perhaps it protests that your project, system design, or art piece isn't finished because it's not perfect yet.

- Perhaps it keeps you from committing to a decision because you're second-guessing the options.

Overthinking can sabotage your success and happiness, paralyzing you with endless doubt and hesitation.

You're not alone in this struggle. Studies show that almost 73% of adults overthink regularly. This widespread issue affects many aspects of life, from career choices to personal relationships. Addressing overthinking is crucial for improving mental health, making better decisions, and building stronger relationships.

This book is for people like you who struggle with overthinking and self-sabotage. You might be dealing with chronic stress, anxiety, and difficulties in making decisions or maintaining relationships. Overthinking can make you second-guess everything, leading to missed opportunities and strained relationships.

The book is divided into several sections. First, we'll explore what overthinking is and how it affects you. We'll examine the science behind it and why it's so common. Next, we'll dive into self-awareness. You'll learn to recognize your overthinking patterns and understand their roots. Then, we'll move on to practical techniques for breaking these patterns. These include mindfulness exercises, decision-making frameworks, and stress-management tools.

Each chapter includes real-life examples to inspire you. You'll also find interactive elements like quizzes, self-assessment tools, and reflection exercises. These will help you apply what you've learned and track your progress.

Engage actively with this book. Take the quizzes, take the self-assessments, and take time for reflection exercises. These tools help you better understand yourself and make real, lasting changes.

A Challenge for You

Have you heard of the 80/20 rule? You might appreciate all the ideas and tools in this book, but I want you to find the 20% that most closely aligns with your needs. Those tools will bring you 80% of the value from reading this book. When you identify them, note them with the phrase "20%."

Change is possible. You *can* silence your mind chatter, make confident decisions, boost your self-confidence, and improve your relationships. Addressing overthinking and self-sabotage can unlock your full potential and lead a more fulfilling life. Let's embark on this journey now.

CHAPTER 1

WHAT IS OVERTHINKING AND ITS IMPACT?

Let's start with a story. It's Monday morning, and you're already dreading the week ahead. Your boss has just assigned you a new project. Instead of feeling excited, your mind starts racing. "Where will I start? What if I can't pull it off? What if the team hates my ideas? What if I make a fool of myself?" By lunchtime, you've concocted an elaborate narrative where you mess up so badly that you get fired, lose your apartment, and end up living under a bridge. Okay, not under a bridge, but you get the idea. This is overthinking.

The Anatomy of Overthinking

Overthinking is like a hamster wheel for your brain. You keep running in circles, but you never actually get anywhere. It's made up of three main elements that work together to create a perfect storm of mental paralysis.

- **Repetitive negative thoughts** are those nagging voices that keep telling you you're not good enough. They replay in your mind like a broken record, making it hard to focus on anything else.

- **Obsessive worrying about the future** occurs when you can't stop thinking about everything that could go wrong. It's like having a personal doomsday prophet living in your head.

- **Endless rumination over past mistakes** keeps you stuck, constantly replaying what you should have said or done differently.

It's crucial to differentiate between **constructive thinking** and **overthinking**.

- Constructive thinking is like a handy Swiss Army knife; it helps you solve problems and make decisions.

- Overthinking, on the other hand, is like trying to use a spoon to cut a steak—completely ineffective and frustrating.

- Constructive thinking involves problem-solving and making plans.

- Overthinking is an unproductive worry that leaves you feeling stuck and anxious.

Common triggers for overthinking include:

- Fear of failure or making mistakes
- Stressful life events
- Uncertainty
- Social and cultural pressures
- High expectations or perfectionism

These triggers set off a chain reaction, leading to a vicious cycle of overthinking:

- *You think about things that could go wrong.*
- **You fear that it will go wrong.**
- *You think about how to prevent it from going wrong.*
- **You worry that's not good enough.**
- *Then you're back at thinking about more things that could go wrong.*

Imagine a day in the life of an overthinker. You wake up worried about an upcoming presentation. Throughout the day, you replay scenarios in your head, imagining all the ways it could go wrong, and by the time you get home, you're emotionally drained but no closer to a solution.

This cycle is self-perpetuating. The more you overthink, the more anxious you become, leading to overthinking. It's a never-ending loop that keeps you stuck. Emotional responses like fear and anxiety fuel this cycle, making it hard to break free.

Take the story of Sarah, an entrepreneur who was paralyzed by decision-making. She had a great business idea but couldn't move forward because she kept second-guessing every decision. "What if I fail? What if people don't like my product?" These thoughts kept her stuck in the planning phase for years.

Or consider Mark, whose relationship was strained by constant worry. He overanalyzed every interaction with his partner, wondering if he said the right thing or was being a good partner. This continuous worry created tension and distance in their relationship.

Exercises

1A. As you continue reading Chapter 1, check off or note those overthinking causes and consequences that apply to you.

- Don't let the lists overwhelm you.

- Remember that the rest of the book is about helping you resolve *your* overthinking.

Overthinking can make you feel like you're carrying the world's weight on your shoulders. But it doesn't have to be this way. By understanding what overthinking is and recognizing its impact, you can start taking steps to break free from its grip, reclaim your mental peace, and unlock your full potential.

Psychological Roots of Overthinking

Cognitive Distortions

Overthinking often sprouts from a tangled web of cognitive distortions, those sneaky little mind tricks that distort reality and make mountains out of molehills.

- **Catastrophizing** is when your brain transforms a minor hiccup into a full-blown disaster movie. You send an email with a typo, and suddenly, you're convinced your boss thinks you're incompetent, which will undoubtedly lead to your termination, financial ruin, and living in your parent's basement. These distorted thinking patterns amplify anxiety and make it nearly impossible to see things clearly.

- **Mind-reading** is when you assume you know what others are thinking. (Spoiler alert: You don't.) You walk into a meeting, see a colleague with a furrowed brow, and immediately think they're judging you. However, they might be feeling ill or lost in their worries.

- **Black-and-white thinking** is the tendency to see things in extremes. Either you're a total success or an utter failure, with no room for the grays in between.

- **Overgeneralization** occurs when one lousy event colors one's entire perspective. For example, if you mess up a presentation, suddenly, you believe you're bad at everything.

EMOTIONAL ISSUES

But cognitive distortions don't operate in a vacuum. They're often fueled by unresolved underlying emotional issues.

- **Anxiety** is a major culprit. It's like a constant background noise that makes you hyper-aware of everything that could go wrong. This heightened state of alertness feeds overthinking, creating a vicious cycle.

- **Low self-esteem** is another driver. When you don't believe in yourself, every decision feels like a potential catastrophe. You doubt your abilities, second-guess your choices, and get stuck in analysis paralysis.

- **Past trauma** is yet another layer that can complicate things. Unresolved trauma can create deeply ingrained thought patterns that make you more prone to overthinking. For example, if you've experienced significant past failures, you might be perpetually haunted by the fear of repeating them. This leads to heightened vigilance and constant mental replay of what could go wrong, making it difficult to move forward.

PERSONALITY TRAITS

Certain personality traits also make some people more susceptible to overthinking.

- **Perfectionism** is a big one. When you set unrealistically high standards for yourself, you're bound to overthink every little detail, fearing that anything less than perfect is a failure.

- **High sensitivity** is another trait that can lead to overthinking. Suppose you're highly attuned to your environment and the emotions of others. In that case, it's easy to become overwhelmed and over-analyze every interaction.

- **Introversion** can also play a role. There's nothing wrong with being introverted, but introverts often spend a lot of time in their heads, which can sometimes tip over into overthinking territory.

MENTAL HEALTH CONDITIONS

Overthinking is often linked with various mental health conditions.

- **Generalized Anxiety Disorder (GAD)** is a big one. People with GAD are chronic worriers, often jumping from one worry to the next without much reprieve.

- **Depression** can also fuel overthinking, making it hard to break free from negative thought patterns.

- **Obsessive-Compulsive Disorder (OCD)** is another condition where overthinking plays a starring role. In OCD, intrusive thoughts can become so overwhelming that they lead to compulsive behaviors aimed at reducing the anxiety caused by these thoughts.

Understanding the psychological roots of overthinking is crucial for addressing it. By recognizing the cognitive distortions, emotional issues, personality traits, and mental health conditions that fuel overthinking, you can start to dismantle its power over you. This book will guide you through practical strategies to tackle these issues head-on.

The Neuroscience Behind Analysis Paralysis

Have you ever wondered why your brain spirals into endless loops of overthinking? It's like a soap opera, with different brain parts playing starring roles.

- Let's start with the **prefrontal cortex**, the brain's CEO. This area is responsible for decision-making, weighing options, and planning. Think of it as the brain's project manager, trying to keep everything organized. But when it gets overloaded, it's like having too many tabs open on your browser. It freezes, and suddenly, you're stuck in analysis paralysis, unable to make even the most straightforward decision.

- Next up is the **amygdala**, the brain's alarm system. It's the part that sounds the "Danger! Danger!" alert when you feel threatened. Its job is to keep you safe, but sometimes it goes overboard. Imagine you're about to give a presentation when your amygdala starts screaming, "What if you mess up? Everyone will laugh at you!" This flood of fear can hijack your brain, making it hard to think clearly.

- Then there's the **hippocampus**, the brain's librarian, responsible for memory recall. It loves to dig up old files and remind you of every mistake you've ever made. When you're about to take a chance, it nudges you and says, "Remember that time in third grade when you tripped during the school play? Yeah, you don't want a repeat of that."

- The **limbic system**, including the amygdala and hippocampus, is the brain's emotional core. It's excellent at processing emotions but can sometimes amplify them, making everything feel more intense than it is.

Neurotransmitters are the brain's chemical messengers and play a massive role in overthinking.

- **Serotonin**, for example, regulates mood. Low levels of serotonin can make you feel anxious and depressed, setting the stage for overthinking.

- Then there's **dopamine**, the brain's reward system. It's the feel-good chemical that motivates you to seek out rewards. However, an imbalance can lead to obsessive thinking, as your brain keeps chasing that elusive "reward" of finding a solution to a non-existent problem.

Neuroplasticity is the brain's ability to change and adapt. It can be a double-edged sword when it comes to overthinking.

- On the one hand, you can rewire your brain to break free from negative thought patterns.

- On the other hand, repetitive overthinking can strengthen those neural pathways, making it a deeply ingrained habit. Think of it like hiking a trail. The more you walk the same path, the more defined it becomes. Similarly, the more you overthink, the stronger those neural pathways get.

Research sheds light on how overthinking impacts the brain.

- Studies on **rumination** show that it's linked to increased activity in the prefrontal cortex and the amygdala, making you more prone to anxiety and depression. Brain imaging in overthinkers reveals heightened activity in these areas, confirming that overthinking isn't just a mental quirk—it's a brain issue.

- **Research** shows chronic stress can shrink the hippocampus, impairing memory and emotional regulation. It also enlarges the amygdala, making you more reactive to stress.

- Evidence links overthinking to mental health disorders like anxiety and depression, creating a vicious cycle that's hard to break.

Understanding the neuroscience behind overthinking gives you a roadmap to tackle it. By recognizing how your brain works, you can start to take control, rewiring those pesky neural pathways and reclaiming your mental peace.

The Emotional Toll of Overthinking

Let's talk about the emotional chaos overthinking can unleash. Imagine waking up daily with a mind that won't shut up. It's like having a noisy neighbor who keeps you up all night, except this neighbor lives in your head.

- Overthinking can lead to **increased anxiety and depression**. When constantly mulling over every possible outcome, your brain gets stuck in a loop of what-ifs and should-haves.

- This mental treadmill not only exhausts you but also sets the stage for **chronic stress and anxiety**.

- **Decreased self-esteem and confidence** are another byproduct of overthinking. When you second-guess every decision, you start to doubt your abilities. You become your worst critic, convinced you're not good enough. This self-doubt can make you feel helpless and frustrated, trapped in a cycle of inaction and regret.

- Over time, the weight of these emotions can become unbearable, leading some to turn to **substance abuse** as a form of escape. It's a desperate, harmful attempt to silence the mind chatter.

The connection between overthinking and mental health issues is well-documented.

- Overthinking can exacerbate existing conditions like **depression and anxiety disorders**. It's a vicious cycle: the more you overthink, the more anxious you become, and the more anxious you are, the more you overthink. This constant state of mental agitation can wreak havoc on your overall well-being.

- Your **sleep suffers**, making it hard to get the rest you need to function properly.

- Lack of sleep, in turn, affects your mood, making you **more irritable and less able to cope with stress**.

Overthinking and emotional distress feed off each other in a never-ending feedback loop.

- Negative emotions like **fear and worry** fuel overthinking, amplifying these emotions. It's like throwing gasoline on a fire. The more you worry, the more reasons you find to worry.

- This is where **confirmation bias** comes into play. Your brain starts seeking information confirming your fears, ignoring anything contradicting them. It's a one-way ticket to a state of perpetual anxiety.

To break this cycle, you need strategies for emotional regulation.

- Mindfulness practices can be incredibly effective. Focusing on the present moment can interrupt the flow of anxious thoughts and bring a sense of calm to your mind.

- Emotional processing exercises are also helpful. These can include journaling your thoughts and feelings, which allows you to externalize them and gain perspective.

- Another technique is deep breathing exercises, which help to activate the body's relaxation response, counteracting the stress response triggered by overthinking.

Consider the story of Emily, a high-achieving software professional who found herself caught in the grip of overthinking. Her constant worry about work performance led to sleepless nights and chronic stress. She started practicing mindfulness, dedicating just ten minutes a day to meditation. This simple practice helped her gain control over her thoughts, reducing her anxiety and improving her sleep. Emotional processing exercises, like writing down and rationalizing her worries, also played a crucial role in her recovery.

Understanding the emotional toll of overthinking is the first step toward reclaiming your mental peace. By implementing strategies for emotional regulation, you can break free from the cycle of worry and regain control over your life.

The Physical Toll of Mental Chatter

Overthinking doesn't just wreak havoc on your mind; it also damages your body. Imagine waking up every morning with a headache that feels like a tiny drummer practicing for a big gig inside your skull.

- Chronic headaches are a common physical symptom of overthinking. Your brain is constantly in overdrive, and tension seeps into your body. The muscles in your neck and shoulders tighten up as if they're bracing for impact. You might rub your temples or massage your neck, but the relief is temporary. The pain comes back because the root cause of your relentless thoughts remains unaddressed.

- Then, the muscle tension and pain pop up out of nowhere. One minute, you're sitting at your desk, and the next, your back feels like it's been twisted into a pretzel. Overthinking can make your muscles tense up, leading to discomfort and even chronic pain. It's like your body is physically manifesting the mental stress you're under.

- You might notice that you clench your jaw or grind your teeth at night. This can lead to more headaches, jaw pain, and even dental issues. It's a vicious cycle that keeps feeding itself.

- Let's not forget about gastrointestinal issues. Your stomach can become a battleground when your mind is in turmoil. Overthinking can lead to a range of digestive problems, from a constant feeling of nausea to more severe issues like irritable bowel syndrome (IBS).

- You might find that your appetite fluctuates wildly; you're either not hungry or can't stop eating.

- Stress hormones like cortisol can wreak havoc on your digestive system, leading to discomfort and irregular bowel movements. It's like your gut is echoing the chaos in your mind.

How does mental stress translate into physical stress?

- When you overthink, your body goes into fight-or-flight mode, even without immediate danger.

- Your brain perceives your thoughts as threats, triggering the release of cortisol.

- This stress hormone prepares your body to fight or flee, but since you're not in danger, it builds up, causing various physical symptoms.

- Over time, this constant alertness leads to mental exhaustion and burnout.

- Your body can't sustain this stress level indefinitely and starts to break down.

The **long-term consequences** of sustained overthinking are serious.

- Chronic stress can increase your risk of cardiovascular diseases.

- Your heart constantly works overtime, leading to high blood pressure and other heart-related issues.

- Your immune system also takes a hit. When your body is constantly in fight-or-flight mode, it doesn't have the resources to fend off illnesses effectively. You might get sick more often or take longer to recover from minor ailments.

Take the story of Jessica, a high-powered banking executive who developed chronic migraines from the constant stress of overthinking at work. Her headaches were so severe that she had to miss important meetings and deadlines, which only fueled her anxiety further.

Or consider Alex, a college student who ended up in the hospital with stomach ulcers. His overthinking about grades and future career prospects led to such severe gastrointestinal issues that he had to take a semester off to recover.

These real-life examples highlight the profound impact of overthinking on physical health. Recognizing the physical toll of overthinking is the first step toward addressing it. By understanding how your mind affects your body, you can start taking steps to alleviate mental and physical stress.

How Overthinking Sabotages Success and Happiness

Let's face it: overthinking is the archenemy of good decision-making. Imagine deciding on something as simple as what to have for dinner. You start with a craving for pizza but then think, "Is pizza healthy? Maybe I should get a salad. But will a salad be satisfying? What if I regret not getting the pizza?" Before you know it, 20 minutes have passed, and you're still staring at the menu, paralyzed by indecision.

Over-reliance on gathering information can make this worse. You might spend hours reading reviews and comparing options, but instead of feeling more confident, you feel more confused. This habit of overanalyzing every choice leads to missed opportunities.

Take my friend Dave, for example. Dave had a fantastic job offer but couldn't decide whether to accept it. He worried about leaving his current role, moving to a new city, and whether the new job would be as fulfilling as it seemed. By the time Dave made up his mind, the offer was gone. His career stagnated because he couldn't make a decision. This is the psychological mechanism at play: cognitive overload and decision fatigue. Your brain gets so overwhelmed with options and potential outcomes that it shuts down, leaving you stuck.

The **paradox of choice** adds another layer of complexity. When faced with too many options, you'd think having more choices would make it easier to find the perfect solution. In reality, it often leads to more anxiety and dissatisfaction. You end up second-guessing your choice, wondering if another option would have been better. This constant questioning is exhausting and unproductive.

Take Stacey, a marketing manager who delayed making a critical decision about a new campaign strategy. She wanted everything to be perfect and kept re-evaluating her options. When she finally chose a direction, the market opportunity had passed, and her company lost out.

Consider James, who missed several career advancements because he couldn't decide whether to apply for higher roles. He was so focused on potential pitfalls that he overlooked the benefits, resulting in missed promotions and financial instability.

Overthinking also torpedoes **productivity**. Picture a day filled with half-finished tasks. You start working on a report but then overthink every detail, questioning whether your approach is correct. You move on to another task, but the same thing happens. By the end of the day, nothing is completed. This is a common scenario for overthinkers. Decreased work efficiency and unfinished tasks become the norm, leading to frustration and stress. You might criticize yourself for procrastination, blaming the wrong issue.

Overthinking can affect professional relationships and career success in the workplace. **Hesitation in communication** makes it difficult to assert yourself. You might struggle to trust colleagues, fearing they'll judge you. This can lead to missed promotions and career advancements. Financial instability often follows as indecision and procrastination impact job performance and growth opportunities.

Consider Lisa, a talented software developer who missed a promotion because she doubted her abilities and didn't apply. Or Tom, who lost his job because he overanalyzed every task, leading to missed deadlines and dissatisfaction from his employer.

The impact on **personal relationships** is equally devastating. Constantly second-guessing interactions can strain friendships and romantic relationships. You might misinterpret a friend's comment, thinking they're upset with you when they're not. This leads to unnecessary conflict and emotional distance. Trust issues arise, and emotional disengagement follows. Overthinking every word and action creates a barrier, preventing genuine connections and intimacy.

My friend Rachel's friendship with her best friend disintegrated because she overanalyzed every interaction, creating misunderstandings and hurt feelings.

Overthinking sabotages success and happiness in countless ways. By recognizing its impact on decision-making, productivity, and relationships, you can take steps to break free from its grip. In the next chapter, we will guide you through practical strategies to reclaim your mental peace and unlock your full potential.

CHAPTER 2

IDENTIFY YOUR OVERTHINKING PATTERNS

I magine you're at a party and just told a joke. You think it's hilarious, but the room goes silent. Cue the mental spiral: "Was it offensive? Did I deliver it wrong? Are they judging me?" This kind of overthinking can turn a fun night into a stress-fueled nightmare.

What if you could pinpoint what sets off this spiral? That's what we're diving into, recognizing your thought triggers.

Recognize Your Thought Triggers

First, let's talk about what triggers those endless loops of worry. Identifying common thought triggers is like finding the root of a pesky weed; you can't get rid of it unless you know where it starts.

Work-related stressors can trigger overthinking. Maybe it's that looming project deadline or the fear of making mistakes during a presentation. These high-pressure situations can send you spiraling into overthinking. You start questioning every detail, wondering if you did enough, and before you know it, you're paralyzed by doubt.

Social interactions can be another big trigger. Do you ever replay a conversation in your head, wondering if you said something wrong? Or worry that people are judging you? This kind of social anxiety can trigger a cascade of overthinking that leaves you feeling insecure and exhausted.

Financial concerns also take a toll. Worrying about bills, savings, and your family's future economic stability can keep your mind racing at night, making it hard to focus on anything else.

These emotional triggers don't just make you feel bad; they activate negative thought patterns that spiral into full-blown anxiety. When you're triggered, your brain goes into overdrive, analyzing every possible outcome, most of which are catastrophic. This connection between emotional triggers and anxiety is why it's so important to identify what sets you off. Once you know your triggers, you can start to manage them.

Monitor Your Triggers

One effective way to pinpoint these triggers is through self-monitoring techniques.

- **Thought Diaries** are a great place to start. Write down your thoughts whenever you feel anxious or start overthinking. Note the situation, your feelings, and any physical sensations. Over time, you'll begin to see patterns.

- A **Trigger Identification Worksheet** can guide you through identifying and analyzing your triggers, making it easier to spot recurring themes. Such a worksheet can include the entries listed below. Copy the sample worksheet shown on the next page or make your own.

    - **Trigger Description:** Briefly describe the situation or event that triggered the overthinking (e.g., receiving a study schedule).

    - **Emotional Response:** List emotions felt when the trigger occurred (e.g., anxiety, frustration, sadness).

    - **Physical Response:** Note any physical sensations or symptoms (e.g., tense muscles, rapid heartbeat).

    - **Behavioral Reaction:** Describe how you reacted at the moment (e.g., avoided studying, procrastinated, or sought reassurance).

    - **Thought Patterns:** Identify specific thoughts or beliefs related to the trigger (e.g., "I'll never be prepared for this exam").

    - **Impact Assessment:** Consider the effect of this trigger on well-being, daily activities, or relationships.

    - **Possible Underlying Beliefs:** Reflect on any beliefs that could influence the reaction (e.g., perfectionism, fear of failure).

    - **Strategy Development:** List practical steps or coping mechanisms to manage or reframe the response next time (e.g., break down the study schedule into manageable tasks and use calming techniques).

- **Outcome Reflection** (for later review): Note if applying the strategy helped reduce overthinking and manage the trigger.

Trigger Identification Worksheet

OVERTHINKING – THE SILENT SABOTEUR ©

Date, time & location	
Trigger Description: situation or event that triggered overthinking	
Emotional Response: felt when triggered	
Physical Response: sensations, symptoms	
Behavioral Reaction: at the moment	
Thought Patterns: thoughts or beliefs related to the trigger	
Impact Assessment: on well-being, daily activities, relationships	
Possible Underlying Beliefs: could influence the reaction	
Strategy Development: steps or coping to manage your response	
Outcome Reflection (later review): whether the strategy helped	

Reflective Journaling Prompts can provide deeper insights. After a recent emotional response, ask yourself, "What was I feeling just before I started overthinking?" or "What triggered this thought pattern?"

- **Apps** for tracking mood and thoughts can be helpful. Apps like **Moodpath** or **Daylio** allow you to log your emotions and thoughts throughout the day, visually representing your mental state.

ANALYZE YOUR TRIGGERS

Once you've gathered some data, it's time to analyze trigger patterns.

- Look for recurring themes in workplace stress. You may notice that tight deadlines always set you off, or it's interactions with a particular colleague.

- In relationships, common themes include fear of rejection or conflict.

- You can more effectively anticipate and manage your trigger reactions by identifying these patterns.

Consider Tara, who struggled with social anxiety. She started keeping a thought diary and realized that her anxiety spiked after social events. By identifying this trigger, she understood that a fear of being judged fueled her overthinking.

Another example is Jake, a college student who continually worried about exams. By using a trigger identification worksheet, he pinpointed that his stress levels soared whenever he received a study schedule. Recognizing this helped him develop strategies to manage his anxiety.

Identifying your thought triggers is the first step in breaking free from the cycle of overthinking. By understanding what sets you off, you can start to take control and reclaim your mental peace.

Assess Yourself: Are You an Overthinker?

Self-awareness is like having a built-in GPS for your mind. It helps you navigate through the labyrinth of thoughts and emotions. But what exactly is self-awareness?

DEFINITION: **Self-awareness** is recognizing and understanding your internal states (emotions, thoughts) and external behaviors (how you interact with the world).

Internal self-awareness is about knowing what you're feeling and why, while external self-awareness involves understanding how others perceive you. High self-awareness can be a game-changer. It allows you to catch yourself in the act of overthinking and redirect your thoughts before they spiral out of control. It also helps regulate your emotions, making it easier to stay calm and composed.

Think about it: when you know your thought patterns, you can interrupt negative cycles before they take over. You start recognizing the triggers and patterns that lead to overthinking, giving you a chance to intervene.

This heightened awareness also makes emotional regulation more manageable. Instead of being swept away by a tide of anxiety or frustration, you become the observer of your mind, capable of steering your emotional ship through stormy seas.

So, how do you determine if you're an overthinker? Self-assessment tools can be incredibly helpful to provide a baseline understanding of your overthinking tendencies.

Exercises

2A. Take the Overthinking Self-Assessment Quiz below, then review the evaluation of your total score.

OVERTHINKING SELF-ASSESSMENT QUIZ

This quiz lists ten statements related to overthinking. Use this scale of one to five to rate how often each statement applies to you:

Hardly Ever – 1
Not Often – 2
Sometimes – 3
Frequently – 4
Almost Always – 5

Write down your rating number for each statement.

1. _____ I find myself constantly replaying past mistakes in my mind.

2. _____ I tend to imagine worst-case scenarios in everyday situations.

3. _____ I often have trouble making decisions because I overanalyze every option.

4. _____ I worry about what others think of me, even after casual interactions.

5. _____ I often revisit decisions I've already made and question whether they were right.

6. _____ I need to plan for every possible outcome, no matter how unlikely.

7. _____ I frequently replay conversations, thinking about what I said or could have said differently.

8. _____ I struggle to stay present because I constantly worry about the future.

9. _____ I tend to set unrealistically high standards for myself and fear not meeting them.

10. _____ I avoid taking action because I worry too much about making the wrong choice.

_____ Add up the rating numbers to get your Total Score.

Find your total score in the following ranges to read your evaluation and recommended action.

Total Score of 10–19: Low Level of Overthinking

Evaluation: You experience occasional overthinking, but it doesn't significantly impact your daily life.

Recommended Action: Keep practicing mindfulness and staying in the moment. Relaxation techniques like meditation and journaling can help you maintain mental clarity and process any creeping tendencies to overthink.

Total Score of 20–29: Moderate Level of Overthinking

Evaluation: You sometimes struggle with overthinking, which may affect your decision-making or cause occasional stress.

Recommended Action: Focus on building healthy habits to manage your thought patterns. Set time limits for decision-making, practice grounding exercises, and break tasks into smaller steps to prevent overthinking from escalating. Consider incorporating self-compassion exercises as well.

Total Score of 30–39: High Level of Overthinking

Evaluation: Overthinking often dominates your thought process, making it difficult to stay present or move forward confidently.

Recommended Action: Use cognitive-behavioral techniques like thought-stopping and reframing negative thoughts to manage overthinking. Incorporate self-compassion exercises to reduce perfectionism and analysis paralysis. A mindfulness routine can also help ground you when thoughts become overwhelming.

Total Score of 40–50: Severe Level of Overthinking

Evaluation: Overthinking is a significant challenge in your life, impacting your ability to relax, make decisions, or feel in control.

Recommended Action: Seek guidance from a therapist or counselor to develop strategies for managing overthinking. Focus on self-awareness, breaking the cycle of negative thoughts, and incorporating daily mindfulness practices. Cognitive Behavioral Therapy (CBT) and relaxation techniques can also be effective in helping you regain control.

Once you have your results, it's crucial to interpret them correctly.

- Understanding where you fall on this spectrum can give you valuable insights into how overthinking impacts your daily life.

- A high level of overthinking can strain personal relationships, making you overly cautious or distant.

- It can also affect professional performance, leading to procrastination and missed opportunities.

Exercises

2B. Review the Overthinking Self-Assessment Checklist below. It lists ten behaviors, each with a name, description, and two recommended solutions. This is not a quiz; it's a checklist.

- Check which of these ten overthinking behaviors apply to you.

- For each one, note its two recommended solutions as possible goals.

Overthinking Self-Assessment Checklist p. 1
OVERTHINKING – THE SILENT SABOTEUR ©

	Behavior	Solutions
1	**Ruminating on Past Mistakes** Continuously replaying past errors and feeling regretful or guilty	• Practice self-compassion by reminding yourself that everyone makes mistakes. • Use cognitive reframing to see mistakes as learning opportunities rather than failures.
2	**Catastrophizing** Always assuming the worst-case scenario will happen	• Challenge negative thoughts by asking yourself, "What evidence do I have that this will happen?" • Practice mindfulness to stay present and avoid getting swept away by future anxieties
3	**Perfectionism** Setting unrealistically high standards for yourself and fearing failure	• Embrace the "good enough" concept and recognize that perfection is unattainable. • Break large tasks into smaller, manageable steps to reduce pressure.
4	**Indecision or Analysis Paralysis** Struggling to make decisions because you overanalyze every option	• Set a time limit for decision-making to avoid endless deliberation. • Focus on the potential positive outcomes of a decision, not just the negative possibilities.
5	**Second-Guessing Yourself** Constantly doubting your decisions and wondering if you made the right choice	• Once a decision is made, trust yourself and avoid revisiting the decision unless new information arises. • Practice self-affirmations to build confidence in your abilities.

Overthinking Self-Assessment Checklist p. 2
OVERTHINKING – THE SILENT SABOTEUR ©

	Behavior	Solutions
6	**People-Pleasing and Worrying About Others' Opinions**	• Recognize that you can't control others' perceptions and prioritize your own values.
—	Overthinking how others perceive you and trying to please everyone	• Set healthy boundaries and accept that not everyone's opinion matters.
7	**Replaying Conversations in Your Head**	• Remind yourself that most people scrutinize conversations less than you do.
—	Overanalyzing every word and gesture from a past interaction	• Focus on future improvements rather than overthinking past conversations.
8	**Overplanning or Trying to Control Every Detail**	• Practice flexibility by acknowledging that not everything can be controlled.
—	Obsessively planning and worrying about all potential outcomes	• Learn to accept uncertainty and embrace adaptability in your plans.
9	**Excessive Worry About the Future**	• Practice grounding exercises to bring your attention back to the present moment.
—	Constantly imagining what could go wrong in future situations	• Create a realistic action plan for the future, then let go of unnecessary worries.
10	**Overthinking Social Interactions**	• Use exposure techniques to get comfortable with discomfort in social situations.
—	Constantly analyzing your behavior or worrying about awkward social moments	• Challenge the assumption that others are judging you harshly.

Consider the story of Lori, a construction executive who struggled with decision-making due to overthinking. By becoming more self-aware, she learned to recognize her mental triggers and interrupt them before they spiraled out of control. This newfound awareness helped her make more confident decisions at work.

Or take John, who managed his anxiety by practicing self-awareness techniques. He started journaling his thoughts and emotions, which helped him identify patterns and triggers. Over time, he gained control over his anxiety, improving both his personal and professional life.

Understanding and assessing your overthinking habits is a powerful first step in reclaiming your mental peace. By becoming more self-aware, you can break free from the cycle of overthinking and lead a more balanced, fulfilling life.

Uncover the Role of Past Experiences in Shaping Your Thought Patterns

Think about the last time you felt an intense rush of anxiety over a seemingly trivial situation. It could be a minor critique from your boss or a casual comment from a friend. Now, ask yourself: why did it hit so hard? These reactions can often be traced back to past experiences that have shaped how we think and respond.

Our core beliefs, which are those deeply ingrained assumptions about ourselves and the world, are formed in our early years.

- Imagine a child who constantly hears they're not good enough. They grow up internalizing this belief, which colors every decision and interaction.

- Early experiences, whether positive or negative, act like blueprints for our future behaviors. They set the stage for how we interpret events and react emotionally.

Significant life events can leave lasting imprints on our thought patterns.

- Consider monumental moments like losing a loved one, earning a major achievement, or experiencing traumatic events. These events can shape our worldview and influence how we handle stress. For example, someone who has faced significant loss might overthink every situation, fearing more loss.

- Unresolved trauma can be a persistent trigger for overthinking. Trauma can create a heightened sense of vigilance, making the brain more prone to overanalyzing situations to protect itself from future harm.

Try some practical exercises to uncover how your past influences your present thought patterns.

Exercises

2C. Guided journaling prompts can be incredibly revealing.

- Ask yourself, "What early memories still affect me today?"
- or "Which past events do I often think about?"

2D. Reflective meditation exercises can also help.

- Spend a few minutes each day focusing on a past experience and observe the emotions and thoughts it brings up.
- This practice can provide insights into how your past shapes your current mindset.

Once you've identified these influences, it's time to reprogram those negative thought patterns.

2E. Start by rewriting your narratives.

- Take a negative belief you hold about yourself and flip the script.
- For example, if you believe you're not good enough, write about all the times you've proven your competence.

2F. Visualizations can also be powerful.

- Imagine yourself healing from past wounds.
- Picture a younger version of yourself and offer them the support and compassion they needed back then.

- This can help reframe your perspective and reduce the emotional charge of past experiences.

Understanding the role of past experiences in shaping your thought patterns can be a transformative step in managing overthinking. Recognizing these influences and reprogramming negative beliefs can create a more balanced and resilient mindset.

Is It Really All-or-Nothing?

Do you ever think, "If I can't do this perfectly, I might as well not do it at all"? That's all-or-nothing thinking, one of the most common cognitive distortions.

DEFINITION: Cognitive distortions are those pestering little mind tricks that warp reality.

They're like fun-house mirrors for your thoughts, making things appear more extreme than they are.

- **Overgeneralization** is another one. It's when you take a single event and turn it into a never-ending pattern of defeat. Miss one deadline, and suddenly, you're convinced you're a failure at everything.

- Then there's **mental filtering**, where you focus solely on the negative aspects of a situation and ignore anything positive.

- These distortions create a distorted reality, making it hard to see things as they truly are.

Impacts

The impact of cognitive distortions on mental health can be profound.

- They're like the background noise in your mind that you can't turn off.

- These distortions feed into anxiety and depression, creating a vicious cycle.

- Constantly filtering out the positive makes it easy to feel hopeless.

- Overgeneralization makes you see setbacks as permanent, fueling feelings of failure.

- All-or-nothing thinking leaves no room for mistakes, adding immense pressure and anxiety.

- These distorted ways of thinking can exacerbate overthinking, turning minor issues into insurmountable problems.

Recognizing your cognitive distortions is the first step in combating them.

Exercises

2G. Start with a cognitive distortions checklist. This tool helps you identify the common distortions you might be falling into.

- For example, do you often find yourself thinking in black-and-white terms?

- Do you dismiss compliments but dwell on criticisms?

2H. Self-assessment exercises can also be helpful.

- Spend a few minutes each day reflecting on your thoughts.

- Write down any distorted thoughts you notice and identify their category.

- This practice can help you become more aware of your mental habits and start to see patterns.

Once you've identified these distortions, it's time to challenge them. **Thought-challenging techniques** are beneficial for this.

2I. Start by questioning the validity of your thoughts.

- Ask yourself, "Is this really true?

- What evidence do I have?"

- Often, you'll find that your thoughts are based more on fear than fact.

2J. Reframing negative thoughts is another effective strategy.

- Instead of thinking, "I always mess up," try, "Sometimes I make mistakes, but I learn from them."

- This shift in perspective can reduce the emotional impact of your thoughts and make them more manageable.

Consider Jane, who struggled with all-or-nothing thinking. She believed that if she couldn't be the best at something, she shouldn't bother trying. This mindset held her back in her career and personal life. Recognizing and challenging this distortion taught her to embrace imperfection and take on new challenges.

Or take Mike, who was prone to catastrophizing. Every minor setback felt like a disaster waiting to happen. Through cognitive-behavioral techniques, he learned to reframe his thoughts and see setbacks as opportunities for growth.

Understanding and challenging cognitive distortions is crucial for breaking the cycle of overthinking. It's about changing the way you perceive situations and react to them. By doing so, you can reduce anxiety, improve your mental health, and lead a more balanced life.

Map Your Overthinking Episodes

Imagine your thoughts are like a sprawling city, and you're trying to navigate it without a map. That's what overthinking feels like—chaotic, overwhelming, and directionless. But what if you had a map?

Thought mapping tools, such as mindmaps and flowcharts, can help you chart your mind's labyrinth, making it easier to identify your thoughts' starting points and paths.

- Mindmaps visually organize your thoughts around a central idea, branching out into sub-thoughts and related concepts. See the following sample mindmap about overthinking in reaction to "my manager asked for changes in my analysis."

- Flowcharts provide a linear progression of your thoughts, showing how one idea leads to another. See the following sample flowchart about overthinking in reaction to your son's missing school project.

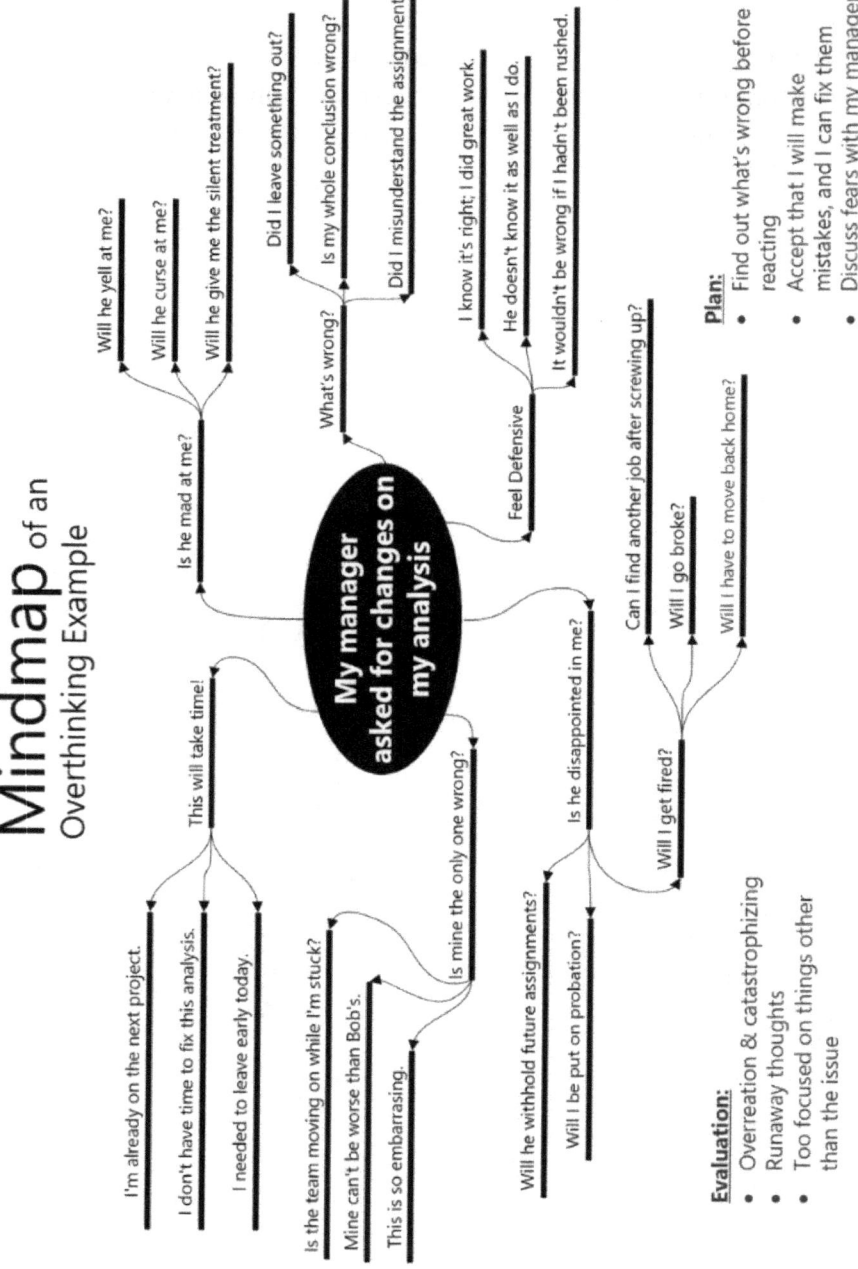

IDENTIFY YOUR OVERTHINKING PATTERNS

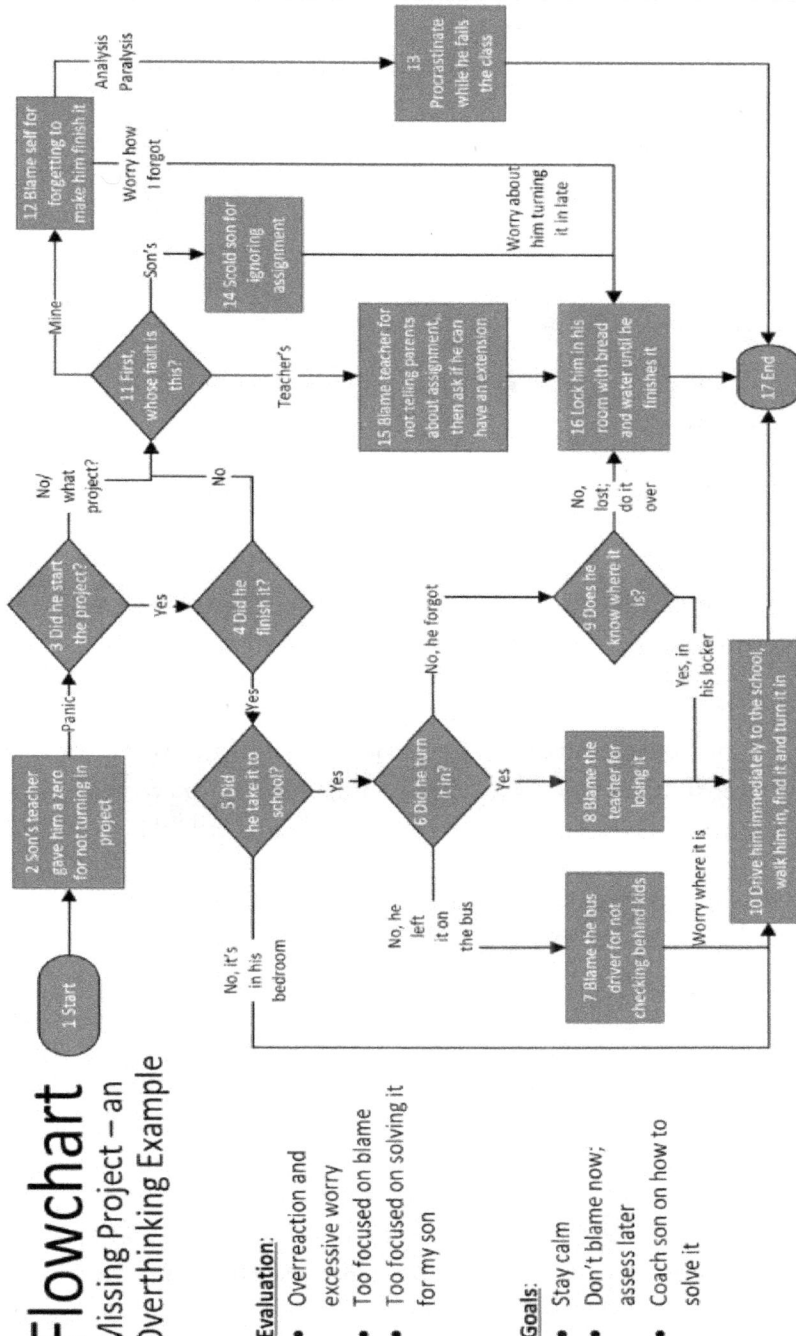

Flowchart
Missing Project – an Overthinking Example

Evaluation:
- Overreaction and excessive worry
- Too focused on blame
- Too focused on solving it for my son

Goals:
- Stay calm
- Don't blame now; assess later
- Coach son on how to solve it

Exercises

2K. Creating a thought map involves a few simple steps.

- Start by identifying the moment an overthinking episode begins. Maybe it's a colleague's comment or an unexpected bill.

- Write this down at the center of your map.

- Next, trace the progression of your thoughts. What's the first thing that comes to mind? Does it trigger another thought?

- Keep branching out, documenting each subsequent thought as it appears.

- This process helps you see the chain reaction that turns a single thought into a full-blown mental spiral.

Analyzing your thought maps can reveal recurring themes and patterns. You might notice that certain situations consistently trigger overthinking.

- For example, work-related thoughts might frequently lead to feelings of inadequacy, while social interactions might trigger worries about acceptance. By identifying these common themes, you can start to understand the underlying issues driving your overthinking.

- Pay attention to the emotional responses linked to these thoughts. Are there specific emotions, like fear, guilt, or frustration, that frequently accompany your overthinking episodes?

Once you've mapped out your thoughts and identified patterns, you can use this information for future planning. **Mindmaps** aren't just diagnostic tools; they can also help you develop action plans to manage overthinking episodes before they spiral out of control.

- For example, if you notice that work-related stress often leads to overthinking, you can create a preventive strategy. This might include setting specific times for work-related tasks, practicing mindfulness during breaks, or seeking colleague feedback to alleviate uncertainties.

Consider Tammy, who struggled with overthinking about her academic performance.

- By mapping her thoughts, she realized that her episodes often started with a poor grade and spiraled into catastrophic thoughts about her academic future.

- With this insight, she developed an action plan. She set up weekly study schedules, practiced mindfulness before exams, and sought regular feedback from her professors.

- These preventive strategies helped her manage overthinking and improve her academic performance.

Mapping your overthinking episodes is like drawing a roadmap through the chaos of your mind. It helps you see where you start, how you get lost, and what paths you can take to find your way out. By understanding the patterns and developing action plans, you can navigate your thoughts more effectively and reduce the impact of overthinking on your life.

Journal for Self-Awareness

Journaling can be a game-changer when it comes to understanding your overthinking patterns. Think of it as a tool to declutter your mind.

- When you put pen to paper, you release pent-up emotions and gain insight into your thought processes.

- It's like having a conversation with yourself, but one where you control the narrative.

- Writing helps you externalize your thoughts, making them more manageable.

- Instead of letting thoughts bounce around in your head, you capture them on the page, where they lose some of their power to overwhelm you.

Different **journaling methods** can aid in self-awareness; there's no one-size-fits-all approach.

- Daily reflection journaling is a great way to track your thoughts and emotions over time. Spend a few minutes each evening jotting down the day's events and your reactions to them.

- Gratitude journaling, on the other hand, focuses on the positive. By listing things you're grateful for, you train your brain to notice the good, which can counteract negative thought patterns.

- Prompt-based journaling offers a more structured approach. Each day, you respond to a specific question or prompt, which can help you explore your thoughts and feelings more deeply.

If you're new to journaling, you might wonder where to start. Practical journaling prompts can guide you.

- For daily reflection, ask yourself, "What was the highlight of my day?" or "What challenged me today?"

- To identify triggers, you might write, "What situation made me feel anxious today?" For reflecting on cognitive distortions, consider, "Did I have any all-or-nothing thoughts today?"

- When processing emotions, you could ask, "How did I feel when X happened, and why?"

Another useful tool is **goal-setting exercises**. Write about what you want to achieve and outline the steps needed.

People often find that journaling helps reduce anxiety and improve decision-making. Take Angie, for instance. She started journaling to manage her anxiety and found that writing about her worries made them feel less daunting. Over time, she noticed patterns in her thoughts and was able to address the root causes of her anxiety.

Then there's Tom, who used journaling to improve his decision-making. By writing out the pros and cons of each choice, he gained clarity and confidence, leading to better outcomes in both his personal and professional life.

Journaling isn't just about writing; it's about discovering yourself. It's a tool for self-awareness that helps you understand your overthinking patterns, identify triggers, and develop healthier ways to cope. The key is consistency, whether you choose daily reflections, gratitude lists, or prompt-based entries. The more you journal, the more insights you'll gain. So grab a notebook and start writing. Your future self will thank you.

Real-Life Case Studies: Overcoming Common Triggers

Let's talk about real people who've managed to break free from the grip of overthinking.

Martina's Story

Take Martina, an IT executive with a paralyzing fear of failure. Every project felt like a test of her worth, and the pressure to succeed was overwhelming. Martina's turning point came when she started practicing mindfulness. She began each day with a ten-minute meditation, focusing on her breathing and letting go of anxious thoughts. Alongside mindfulness, she incorporated cognitive-behavioral techniques. She challenged her negative thoughts by asking, "What evidence do I have that I'll fail?" Gradually, Martina learned to trust herself. As a result, she became more decisive, her confidence soared, and she began leading projects with a newfound sense of calm.

Wayne's Story

Then there's Wayne, who struggled with social anxiety. When attending a networking event, simple interactions felt like climbing Mount Everest. Wayne's breakthrough came through a combination of exposure therapy and reflective journaling. He started small, attending events for just 15 minutes, gradually increasing his time as he grew more comfortable. Journaling allowed him to process his experiences and recognize patterns in his anxiety. He also used cognitive-behavioral techniques to reframe his thoughts, replacing "Everyone is judging me" with "People are focused on themselves, not scrutinizing me." Over time, Wayne's social anxiety diminished. He became more confident in social settings, which improved his work relationships and reduced his overall stress.

The strategies these individuals used can be incredibly effective.

- **Mindfulness practices**, like meditation, help ground you in the present moment, reducing the power of anxious thoughts.

- **Cognitive-behavioral techniques** are equally powerful, enabling you to challenge and reframe negative thought patterns.

- Combining these approaches can lead to significant improvements in both mental clarity and emotional well-being.

Benefits

The long-term benefits of overcoming overthinking triggers are profound.

- Increased confidence and better decision-making skills are just the beginning.

- Your relationships will improve as you become more adept at managing your thoughts.

- You'll find it easier to communicate openly and honestly, reducing misunderstandings and building stronger connections.

- The overall stress reduction will enhance your quality of life, making you more resilient in facing challenges.

Learning from our case studies can provide practical tips for your journey.

- Start with small, manageable steps. If mindfulness seems daunting, begin with just five minutes a day.

- Use cognitive-behavioral techniques to challenge your negative thoughts.

- Remember, progress takes time, and it's okay to have setbacks. What matters is that you keep moving forward.

Inspirational quotes can also be a source of motivation.

> *The only limit to our realization of tomorrow is our doubts of today.*
> Franklin D. Roosevelt

Reflect on this as you work through your triggers. By addressing overthinking, you unlock your full potential and lead a more fulfilling life.

The next chapter will explore how to break free from analysis paralysis and make confident decisions. Your overthinking patterns are just the beginning. Let's dive into actionable strategies to reclaim your mental peace and boost your decision-making skills.

Chapter 3

Break Free from Analysis Paralysis

Imagine this: you're at a crossroads in your career, trying to decide whether to stay in your current role or take a leap into a new opportunity. You've made a pros and cons list, talked to friends, and even consulted your horoscope, but you're still stuck. The clock is ticking, and indecision is gnawing at you.

We've all been there. Analysis paralysis can make even the most straightforward decisions feel like complex puzzles. But what if there were frameworks that could help simplify the process and bring clarity? This is where we'll review decision-making frameworks, your new best friends.

Use Decision-Making Frameworks

Using structured decision-making frameworks can dramatically simplify your life.

Eisenhower Matrix

Let's start with the Eisenhower Matrix, a task management tool that helps you prioritize tasks based on urgency and importance.

- Visualize a grid like the one shown here which is divided into four quadrants.

- The horizontal axis depicts urgency, ranging from less urgent on the left to more urgent on the right.

- The vertical axis shows importance, ranging from less important at the bottom to more important at the top.

- Quadrant 1 is the top right square, representing urgent and important tasks, like finishing a project with a tight deadline.

- Quadrant 2 is the top left square, representing important but not urgent tasks, such as long-term planning or professional development.

- Quadrant 3 is the bottom right square representing urgent but not important tasks, like answering non-critical emails.

- Quadrant 4 is the bottom left square representing tasks that are neither urgent nor important, like scrolling through social media.

- By categorizing tasks, you can focus on what truly matters and delegate or eliminate the rest.

Decision Trees

Next up are Decision Trees. Picture a flowchart like the one shown on the next page. It starts with a single decision point and branches into various outcomes based on different choices. Each branch represents a possible path, helping you visualize the consequences of each option. For example, suppose you're deciding where to relocate after college for a job. In that case, your decision tree might include branches for job offers received, affordability, and career growth. This visual representation can make complex decisions more manageable by breaking them down into bite-sized pieces.

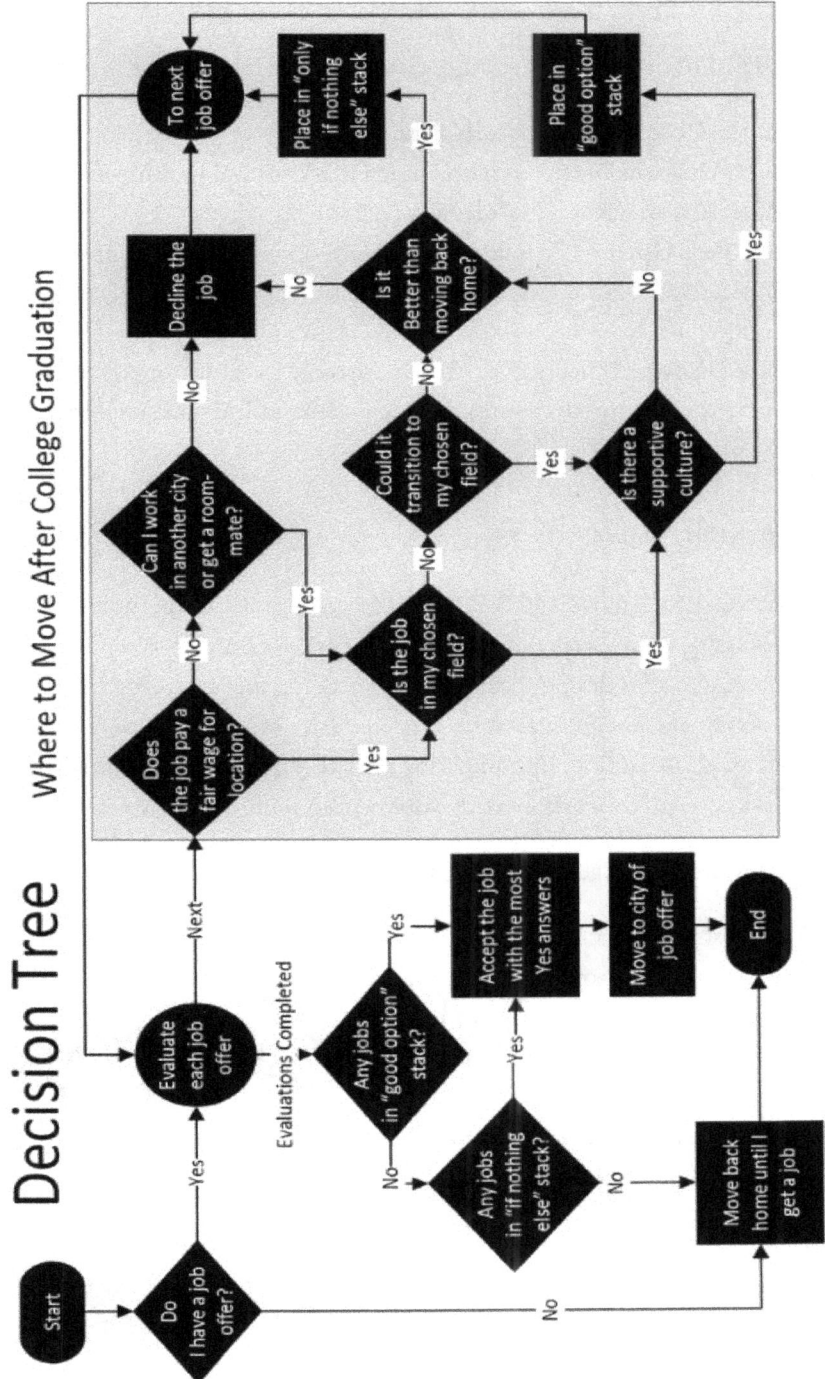

DECIDE Framework

The DECIDE framework is another powerful tool. It stands for these steps.

Define the Problem: First, clearly define the problem you're facing.
Establish Criteria: Next, establish criteria that the ideal solution should meet.
Consider Alternatives: Consider all possible alternatives.
Identify Best Option: Then identify the best option that fits your criteria.
Develop Action Plan: Develop a detailed action plan to implement your decision.
Evaluate Decision: Finally, evaluate the outcome to learn from the experience. This structured approach ensures you cover all bases and make well-informed decisions.

Cost/Benefit Analysis

A **Cost/Benefit Analysis (CBA)** is another tried-and-true method. This involves listing all the costs and benefits associated with each option. For example, suppose you're considering starting a side hustle. In that case, you'd list costs like time, money, and energy against benefits like extra income, skill development, and personal satisfaction. By comparing the two, you can determine whether the benefits outweigh the costs, making your decision more transparent.

There are two challenges with using a CBA.

1. Some costs might be one-time only while benefits are ongoing, so consider a 5-year or 10-year projection. The point at which you "break even" and start earning a profit can be in a future year. This multi-year projection can be further complicated by factoring in the time value of the money.

2. Many benefits like your happiness or customer satisfaction are very difficult to put a dollar value on. If you're preparing a CBA for a small business loan application, be sure you can explain your assumptions about these factors.

SWOT Analysis

Lastly, let's talk about **SWOT Analysis**, shown here, which companies often use to evaluate their product's position relative to their competition. This acronym stands for **Strengths, Weaknesses, Opportunities**, and **Threats**. This framework helps you evaluate an option from multiple perspectives. 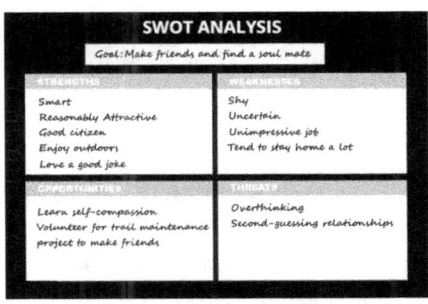 Suppose you are considering returning to college for a higher-level degree. You'd list your strengths (e.g., skills and experience), weaknesses (e.g., lack of a competitive degree), opportunities (e.g., job market trends for people with a higher level of education), and threats (e.g., long-term career prospects without the advanced degree, and paying back a student loan). This analysis doesn't provide a bottom-line summation, but this holistic view can provide valuable insights and highlight areas that need attention.

The benefits of using these frameworks are immense. They reduce mental clutter by providing a clear structure for decision-making. Instead of feeling overwhelmed by options, you can focus on what's important. These frameworks enhance clarity and confidence, making it easier to move forward. Establishing criteria for decision-making is crucial. Set clear objectives and list your priorities. Differentiate between essential and non-essential criteria to streamline your choices.

Exercises

3A. Create a personal Eisenhower Matrix for your daily tasks.

- Categorize your to-do list into the four quadrants and focus on what's truly important.

3B. Create a SWOT Analysis for a career decision.

- List your strengths, weaknesses, opportunities, and threats to gain a comprehensive view.

These exercises will help you internalize the frameworks and make them second nature.

Integrating these structured approaches into decision-making allows you to overcome analysis paralysis and make confident, informed choices.

Overcome the Fear of Making Mistakes

Imagine standing on the edge of a cliff, peering down at the vast unknown below. That's what the fear of making mistakes feels like. It's paralyzing, leaving you stuck in place, afraid to take the next step.

- This fear is often rooted in the fear of judgment from others. We worry that making mistakes will expose us to ridicule, criticism, or rejection.

- Perfectionism fuels this fear, leading to avoidance. If you believe anything less than perfect is a failure, you will likely avoid taking risks altogether.

- Past negative experiences also play a significant role. If you've been burned before, the memory of that pain can make you hesitant to try again.

Mistakes Are Learning Opportunities

How can you manage this fear? Reframe mistakes as learning opportunities.

- Instead of seeing a mistake as a catastrophe, view it as a chance to grow. Ask yourself, "What can I learn from this?"

- Mindfulness practices can also help reduce anxiety. Staying present can prevent your mind from spiraling into worst-case scenarios.

- Techniques like deep breathing and meditation can calm your nerves, making it easier to face potential mistakes with a clearer mind.

Take Melinda, for example. She was an insurance professional who lived in constant fear of making mistakes. Her turning point came when she decided to embrace failure. She started small, taking on tasks with a low risk of failure, and gradually worked her way up. Each time she made a mistake, she analyzed it, learned from it, and moved on. Her confidence grew, and she took on bigger challenges at work.

Consider Paul, a college student who struggled with academic setbacks. He used to see every low grade as a reflection of his abilities. But by reframing these setbacks as learning opportunities, he improved his study habits and eventually excelled in his courses.

Action Steps

Here are some actionable steps to start facing your fear of mistakes.

- First, challenge your negative thoughts. When you think, "I'm going to fail," ask yourself, "What evidence do I have for this?" Often, you'll find that your fears are based more on anxiety than fact.

- Next, set small, achievable goals. Instead of aiming for perfection, focus on making incremental progress. This can help build your confidence and reduce the pressure to be perfect.

- Practicing self-compassion and positive self-talk is also crucial. Remind yourself that everyone makes mistakes and that they don't define your worth.

- Lastly, try behavioral experiments to test fear-related beliefs. If you're afraid of speaking up in meetings, start by making small comments and gradually increase your participation. You'll likely find that your fears are unfounded, and each small success will build your confidence.

Simplify Complex Choices

Imagine staring at a decision that feels like trying to solve a Rubik's cube while blindfolded. Complex choices can be overwhelming, but breaking them down into manageable parts can make them easier to tackle.

Start by **identifying the core components** of the decision. For example, if you're contemplating a career change, the core components might include financial implications, job satisfaction, work-life balance, and long-term career growth. By isolating these elements, you can focus on each one separately, making the overall decision less daunting.

Using **flowcharts to visualize decision paths** can also be incredibly helpful. Picture a flowchart with your decision at the top. Each branch represents a different option, with sub-branches detailing potential outcomes and consequences. This visual representation allows you to see the decision's complexity laid out in a structured way, helping to reduce the mental clutter that comes with overthinking.

Prioritization is another key concept in overcoming analysis paralysis. Prioritizing tasks and decisions means determining what needs immediate attention and what can wait. It's about differentiating between urgent and important tasks. Urgent tasks demand immediate action, while important tasks contribute to long-term goals but don't necessarily require immediate attention. This distinction is critical because it helps you focus on what matters rather than getting bogged down by less significant details.

Several prioritization techniques can guide you.

- The **Pareto Principle**, or the **80/20 Rule**, suggests that 80% of your results come from 20% of your efforts. Identify that 20%—those high-impact actions—and prioritize them.
  - If you are starting a side business, personally selling your product or service will fall in the 20% of efforts driving your results, while advertising through flyers might not.
- The **Eisenhower Matrix** discussed earlier is another effective tool for

distinguishing between urgent and important tasks.

- If you're starting a side business, selling and fulfilling your product or service can be classified as Important and Urgent because you can't make money without it.

- Obtaining a business license might be Urgent, but it's Not Important that *you* do it; you could delegate it.

- Tracking your income and expenses will be Important but not Urgent, so it could be delegated or done after selling and fulfilling.

- In the digital age, printing business cards is likely not urgent and not important.

• The **M S C W Method** is typically called the Moscow Method. It categorizes tasks into <u>**M**ust have</u>, <u>**S**hould have</u>, <u>**C**ould have</u>, and <u>**W**on't have</u>, helping you focus on what's most critical. In your side business, you might classify the following.

- <u>Must Have</u>: Primary product or service to sell

- <u>Should Have</u>: A web presence to market your product or service, making it known

- <u>Could Have</u>: A website that sells your product or service, processing the financial payment

- <u>Won't Have</u>: A storefront to physically sell your product or service (because this is a side business, not full-time, and the cost/benefit analysis doesn't justify it)

• A **Weighted Decision Matrix** assigns different weights to each criterion based on its importance, providing a clear numerical value for each option. Assume you're evaluating multiple job opportunities and want to assign numeric values to potential answers.

- You can start with this point system for your answers: Great = 4, Good = 3, Fair = 2, Not good = 1, Never = 0.

- For job satisfaction, you might assign a weight of 10, multiplying each job opportunity's answer by ten as the weight factor. An answer of "Great" would be 40 (4x10), and "Fair" would be 20 (2x10).

- For the climate of a relocation city, you might assign a weight of 1, so when the answer is multiplied by 1, it doesn't increase. "Great" remains a 4, and "Fair" remains a 2.

- For your partner's willingness to move to a relocation city, you might assign a weight of 5, multiplying each job opportunity's answer by five as the weight factor. An answer of "Great" would be 20 (4x5), and "Fair" would be 10 (2x5).

- After the answers to all questions for each job opportunity are added up, the weighted answers will substantially impact the results in proportion to their weights.

Benefits

Simplifying choices has immense benefits.

- It reduces cognitive load, making it easier to process information without feeling overwhelmed.

- Simplification enhances focus, allowing you to concentrate on critical factors and make more informed decisions.

- You'll find that breaking down complex choices makes the decision-making process more manageable and increases your confidence in your choices.

Consider the case of Sunitha, who was overwhelmed by the decision to switch careers. She tackled each aspect individually by breaking down the decision into the important core components—salary, job satisfaction, and growth opportunities. She used a Weighted Decision Matrix to assign importance to each criterion and visualize the best option. This approach helped her make a confident, informed decision in alignment with her long-term goals.

Exercises

3C. To practice simplifying complex choices, try a Weighted Decision Matrix exercise for a personal decision you're facing. If you don't have one, then make one up.

- List the choices that you're deciding between, such as the job opportunities, houses to buy, or baby names

- Select the criteria that you want to consider for each choice. You might include the criteria described in the explanation above for job opportunities. For which house to buy, include whether it meets your required number of bedrooms and bathrooms. For baby names, include compatibility with a last name, family tradition, and not getting teased at school.

- Choose a series of potential answers and assign base number values to them, such as the 4, 3, 2, 1, and 0 used in the explanation above.

- For each potential choice, select answers for each criterion and list its assigned numeric value with the answer.

- Assign weights to each criterion based on what's more important to you, and multiply the weight factor by the criterion's answer for each choice.

- Sum up the scores for each choice and see which choice has the highest score.

- This exercise will help you see how simplification can lead to clearer, more confident decisions.

Build Confidence in Your Decisions

Imagine standing in the fog, unable to see the way forward. That's what decision-making often feels like when confidence is lacking. **Confidence** is the lighthouse of effective decision-making. It brings mental clarity, cutting through the fog of doubt and indecision. When you're confident, your mind isn't cluttered with the fog of "what ifs" and worst-case scenarios. You see the options clearly and choose based on rational thought rather than fear.

Confidence also propels personal and professional growth. It encourages you to take risks, seize opportunities, and step out of your comfort zone. Without it, stagnation becomes the norm, and growth remains a distant dream.

Building and maintaining decision-making confidence doesn't happen overnight, but it's doable with the proper techniques.

- Visualization is a powerful method. Picture yourself successfully navigating a challenging decision. See the positive outcome and feel the relief and satisfaction. This mental rehearsal prepares your brain for success, making it easier to act confidently when the time comes.

- Positive affirmations are another tool. Start your day by telling yourself, "I am capable of making good decisions," or "I trust myself to choose wisely." These affirmations might feel cheesy at first, but they can rewire your brain to support, rather than sabotage, your confidence.

Consider the story of Tim, a process improvement professional who struggled with decision-making. He constantly doubted his choices, fearing failure at every turn. Through visualization exercises, he began to see himself making successful recommendations. He complemented this with positive affirmations, telling himself daily that he had the skills and insight to succeed. Over time, his confidence grew. He became more decisive, and his career thrived.

Take Marcie, a software sales professional who gained self-assurance through practice. She started small, making low-stakes decisions quickly and confidently.

Each success, no matter how minor, built her confidence. Soon, she was tackling more significant decisions with the same level of assurance.

Exercises

3D. To start building your confidence, try creating a decision-making journal.

- Document your choices, the steps you took, and the outcomes.

- Reflect on what went well and what you can improve.

This process provides tangible evidence of your decision-making abilities.

3E. Another practical step is setting up a support system.

- Seek feedback from trusted friends, family, or colleagues. Their encouragement and insights can bolster your confidence and provide a safety net as you navigate complex decisions.

- When you know you have a team cheering you on, the fear of making a wrong choice diminishes. You feel empowered to act, knowing you have a network to lean on even if things don't go as planned.

Use Pros and Cons Lists Effectively

Imagine you're standing at a crossroads, unsure which path to take. You're weighing the options, but they all blur together, each with its challenges and rewards. This is where a list of pros and cons can be a game-changer.

DEFINITION: The terms ***pro*** and ***con*** come from Latin. The Latin word *pro* means "for" or "in favor of," and *con* is derived from the Latin *contra*, meaning "against."

A pros and cons list for each option is a simple yet powerful decision-making tool that helps you visualize which option is better. Listing the advantages and disadvantages of each option gives you a clearer picture of that option's potential impact. This visual representation can cut through the mental clutter, making it easier to see the forest and the trees.

Trade in old car for new one	
Pros	Cons
New warranty	Car payments
Better gas mileage	Higher insurance
Newer safety features	Don't have $ for a down-payment

Keep old car	
Pros	Cons
No car payment	Could need transmission work
Low car insurance	Worth more now on trade-in than at 140K miles
Can get another 50K miles	Needs a paint job

Creating an effective pros and cons list starts with brainstorming and categorizing your thoughts. Grab a piece of paper or open a digital document and write one of your options at the top as a title. Draw a line down the middle. Label the left side of the line as "Pros" and the right side as "Cons." Begin by listing that option's positive aspects under "Pros" and the negative aspects under "Cons." Be thorough and objective. It's easy to let biases sneak in, so make sure you're considering all angles. For example, deciding whether to change careers should include job satisfaction, salary, commute, work-life balance, and growth opportunities. The more comprehensive your list, the better. Then repeat this pros and cons list for your next option until each option has been evaluated.

Once you've created your lists, it's time to analyze and weigh the pros and cons. Not all factors are created equal, so assign weights to different elements based on their importance. For example, if work-life balance is crucial to you, give it a higher weight than a minor inconvenience like a longer commute. Consider both short-term and long-term impacts. Something that seems like a big deal now might matter less in the future, and vice versa. This weighted approach can help you see which option provides the most significant overall benefit.

Let's look at a couple of specific examples. Say you're contemplating a career change. Under "Pros," you might list a higher salary, better work-life balance, and growth opportunities. Under "Cons," you could include the risk of the unknown, the potential need for additional education, and leaving a comfortable routine. Assign weights to each factor based on their importance to you.

Another example could be deciding whether to purchase a replacement for your car. Pros could include better fuel efficiency, lower maintenance costs, and improved safety features. Cons could be the upfront cost, potential depreciation, and financing terms.

A well-crafted pros and cons list can be a lifeline in indecision. You can make more informed and confident choices by breaking your options into clear, visual elements.

EXERCISES

3F. Create and evaluate a Pros and Cons list for a decision you must make.

LEARN HOW TO TRUST YOUR GUT INSTINCTS / INTUITION

Gut instincts often feel like a whisper from deep inside, guiding you when logic seems murky. They're also called intuition. But what exactly fuels these feelings? It's all about the subconscious mind. Think of your subconscious as a massive storage room for every experience, emotion, and piece of knowledge you've ever encountered. When you encounter a situation, your subconscious sorts through this vast archive at lightning speed, connecting dots you might not consciously see.

Past experiences play a crucial role here. Suppose you've been in a similar situation before. In that case, your gut instinct draws on that memory, nudging you towards a decision based on what worked or didn't work previously. It's a blend of neural connections firing rapidly and emotional memories bubbling to the surface, creating that intuitive hunch.

But how do you tune into these instincts when your mind is a cacophony of thoughts?

- Practicing mindfulness can help. By staying present, you quiet the mental noise, making it easier to hear that inner voice.

- Simple techniques like deep breathing or a short meditation session can enhance self-awareness, allowing you to connect more clearly with your intuitive feelings.

- Reflective exercises are another tool. Journal for a few minutes daily about your decisions and how they felt.

- Over time, you'll notice patterns and develop a stronger connection with your inner wisdom.

Intuition and rational analysis have their place in decision-making; the trick is knowing when to rely on each. Intuition is often most useful when making quick decisions or when the data is incomplete. It's that immediate sense of what feels right. Rational analysis, on the other hand, is crucial for decisions that require a thorough examination of facts and figures. One technique for balancing the two is starting with intuition and then using rational analysis to validate or challenge it. For example, if your gut tells you a business opportunity is promising, research to see if the numbers back it up. This way, you combine the best of both worlds.

Consider the story of Takesha, the VP of R&D at a service company who trusted her gut in a high-stakes situation. Faced with a critical decision about expanding the company, Takesha felt an intuitive pull towards a particular market. While the rest of the leadership team hesitated, Takesha's gut told her it was the right move. She combined this instinct with a thorough market analysis, and the expansion was a huge success.

Take Patrick, who relied on his gut to make a personal relationship decision. He had been dating someone for a while but felt something was off. He trusted his intuition and decided to end the relationship, which later proved to be the right choice as he found someone who truly aligned with his values.

Exercises

3G. Think about a time when your gut instinct or intuition seemed to be telling you something.

- What did you think about receiving guidance from such a source?

- Did you try to prove or disprove the advice?

- Did you follow that advice?

- Did you make the right decision?

Trusting your gut can be a powerful tool in your decision-making arsenal. By understanding the science behind intuition, cultivating mindfulness, and balancing it with rational analysis, you can make decisions that feel both right and reasoned.

Real-Life Case Studies of Successful Decision-Making

Carla's Story

Imagine you're a small business owner like Carla, who faced a critical decision about whether to expand her bakery. Carla loved her cozy shop but sensed a growing demand for her unique pastries.

- The pressure to make the right move was intense.

- She started by identifying key decision points: location, investment cost, and potential revenue.

- Carla then conducted a risk assessment, weighing the benefits of increased sales against the financial risks.

- She sought advice from a business mentor and conducted a market analysis.

- Her flexibility and willingness to adapt were crucial.

- Carla decided to open a second location, and it was a huge success, doubling her revenue within a year.

- The key takeaway? Flexibility and the courage to seek advice can pave the way for successful decision-making.

Eric's Story

Let's look at a student named Eric, who was torn between two academic paths: engineering and graphic design. Both had their merits, but Eric felt paralyzed by the fear of choosing the wrong path.

- He began by identifying his core interests and career goals.

- Eric then analyzed the risks, considering job stability, potential income, and personal satisfaction.

- He spoke with professionals in both fields and even shadowed them for a day. This firsthand experience provided invaluable insights.

- Eric also consulted academic advisors and used their input to refine his decision.

- Ultimately, he chose graphic design, a field where he felt more passionate and creative.

- The lesson here is clear: seeking input from various sources and gaining firsthand experience can significantly aid in making informed decisions.

These case studies highlight the importance of **identifying key decision points** and **conducting thorough risk assessments**.

- Carla and Eric both demonstrated the value of flexibility and adaptability. They were open to changing their plans based on new information and advice.

- This mindset reduced their anxiety and led to better outcomes.

- Seeking input from mentors, professionals, and advisors gave them diverse perspectives, enriching their decision-making process.

One practical insight from these stories is the **balance between intuition and rationality**.

- Carla trusted her gut feeling about the market demand but backed it up with thorough research and advice.

- Eric felt pulled toward graphic design but validated his choice through shadowing and consultations.

- This balance can help you navigate uncertainty and ambiguity.

Another technique is to break down the decision into smaller, manageable parts.

- Carla tackled location and investment separately.

- Eric focused on interests and job prospects individually.

Handling uncertainty involves accepting that no decision is without risk. Carla and Eric embraced the unknown, understanding that some ambiguity is inevitable. They took calculated risks, informed by their research and advice. This approach can minimize the fear of making mistakes and boost your confidence in your choices.

In the next chapter, we'll explore how to silence mind chatter.

CHAPTER 4

SILENCE MIND CHATTER WITH PRACTICAL TECHNIQUES

Picture this: You're driving home after a long day and suddenly remember that awkward thing you said in a meeting five years ago. Your mind starts spiraling, replaying every cringe-worthy moment in excruciating detail. Sound familiar? Overthinking can strike at any time, turning your brain into a hamster wheel of anxiety. But what if there was a way to hit the brakes and find mental peace? We can turn to mindfulness, a powerful tool for gaining mental clarity and silencing that relentless mind chatter.

Adopt Mindfulness Techniques for Mental Clarity

Mindfulness might sound like a buzzword, but it's been around for centuries, rooted in ancient meditation practices. At its core, mindfulness is about being fully present in the moment, aware of where you are and what you're doing, without being overly reactive or overwhelmed by your surroundings. It's like giving your brain a much-needed vacation from the constant barrage of thoughts.

Definition: Jon Kabat-Zinn, a pioneer in mindfulness-based stress reduction, defines **mindfulness** as "awareness that arises through paying attention, on purpose, in the present moment, non-judgmentally."

The origins of mindfulness trace back to Buddhist traditions, but it's not about religion—it's about mental well-being. Imagine sitting quietly and observing your thoughts like clouds passing by. You don't judge them; you simply notice and let them float away. This practice can reduce stress, improve concentration, and even remodel the physical structure of your brain. You read that right; mindfulness can change your brain, boosting creativity and strengthening neural connections.

Exercises

Let's dive into some practical mindfulness exercises to help you get started.

4A. One of the most popular techniques is the **body scan meditation**.

- Find a quiet space and a comfortable position—sitting or lying down.
- Close your eyes and take a few deep breaths.
- Start by focusing on your toes and noticing any sensations.
- Gradually move your attention up through your body, part by part, until you reach the top of your head.

- This exercise helps you tune into your body and brings your mind into the present moment.

4B. Another powerful practice is **loving-kindness meditation**.

- Sit comfortably and close your eyes.
- Take a few deep breaths and bring someone you care about to mind.
- Silently repeat phrases like, "May you be happy. May you be healthy. May you be safe."
- Gradually extend these wishes to yourself, loved ones, and even people you find challenging.
- This practice cultivates compassion and reduces negative emotions.

4C. Guided imagery is another technique that can transport you to a calm place.

- Close your eyes and imagine a peaceful scene, such as a beach, a forest, or a cozy room.
- Engage all your senses: feel the sand between your toes, hear the rustling leaves, smell the fresh air.
- Guided imagery can reduce stress and create a sense of tranquility.

4D. Mindful eating is a simple yet effective way to bring mindfulness into your daily routine.

- Next time you eat, slow down and savor each bite.
- Notice the flavors, textures, and aromas.
- Pay attention to how your body feels as you eat.
- This practice enhances your enjoyment of food and helps you develop a healthier relationship with eating.

The science behind mindfulness is fascinating. Research shows that mindfulness impacts the brain in profound ways. It strengthens the prefrontal cortex, the area responsible for decision-making and self-control, making it easier to manage overthinking. Mindfulness also reduces activity in the amygdala, the brain's fear center, which means less anxiety and stress. Regularly practicing mindfulness can rewire your brain to be more resilient and focused.

Daily Usage

Incorporating mindfulness into your daily life can be as simple as setting reminders for mindful moments.

- Start with short sessions, perhaps five minutes daily, and gradually increase the duration as you become more comfortable.

- Practice mindfulness during daily routines, like brushing your teeth or walking to work.

- Use apps and recordings for guided sessions—many are available for free and can provide structure and support as you develop your practice.

Mindfulness isn't about achieving a state of perpetual zen. It's about waking up to your life, moment by moment, and finding peace amidst the chaos. By adopting mindfulness techniques, you can silence the mind chatter, reduce overthinking, and gain mental clarity. So, the next time you find yourself spiraling into a thought loop about that embarrassing moment from years ago, take a deep breath, ground yourself in the present, and let those thoughts float away like clouds in the sky.

Use Guided Breathing Exercises for Instant Calm

Imagine sitting in a meeting, your heart racing, your palms sweaty, and your mind spiraling out of control. We've all been there. The beauty of controlled breathing is that it can quickly calm your mind and body. Breathing is directly connected to the autonomic nervous system, which controls your fight-or-flight response. By regulating your breathing, you can signal to your brain that it's okay to relax. This simple act can reduce stress, lower blood pressure, and improve mood.

Let's dive into some specific breathing techniques that can help.

Box breathing, also known as the 4-4-4-4 technique, is a professional favorite. This method helps to regulate your breath, calm your nervous system, and focus your mind. A diagram is included here for visual learners.

- Sit comfortably and inhale deeply through your nose for a count of four.

- Hold your breath for four counts.

- Then, exhale slowly for another four counts.

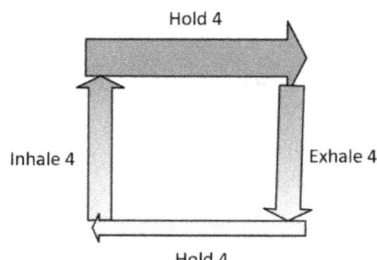

- Hold your breath again for four counts before starting the cycle over.

Diaphragmatic breathing, or belly breathing, is another powerful technique. This type of breathing engages the diaphragm, improving oxygen exchange and calming the nervous system.

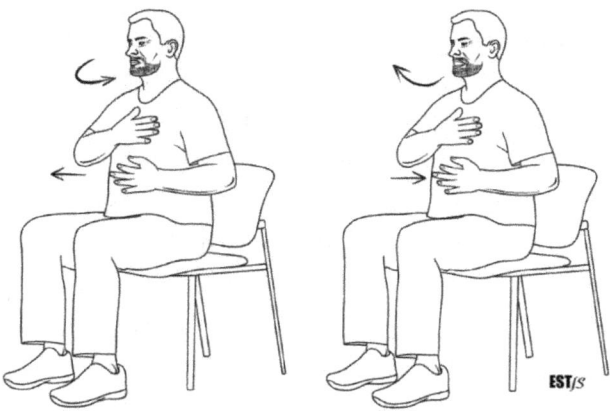

- Lie or sit comfortably and place one hand on your chest and the other on your abdomen.

- Inhale deeply through your nose, allowing your diaphragm to inflate like a balloon. Your hand on your abdomen should rise, while the hand on your chest should remain relatively still.

- Exhale slowly through your mouth.

The **4-7-8 breathing technique** can be a lifesaver for those moments of acute anxiety. This method slows your heart rate and promotes a sense of calm, making it perfect for high-stress situations. A diagram is included here for visual learners.

- Sit or lie down comfortably. Inhale through your nose for a count of four,

- Hold your breath for seven counts,

- Then, exhale slowly through your mouth for eight counts.

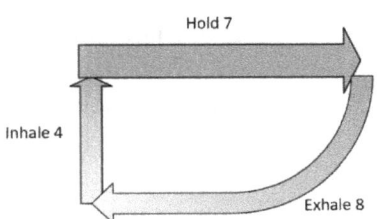

Alternate nostril breathing is another technique worth trying. This exercise balances the body's energy and calms the mind.

- Sit comfortably and use your right thumb to close your right nostril.

- Inhale deeply through your left nostril.

- Close your left nostril with your ring finger and release your right nostril.

- Exhale through the right nostril.

- Then, inhale through the right nostril.

- Close the right nostril again and release your left nostril.

- Exhale through the left nostril.

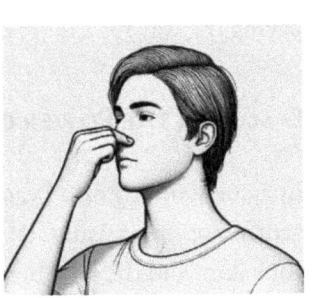

Many people have found these techniques incredibly effective. Take Ramya, a busy technology professional who uses box breathing before every presentation. She says it helps her stay calm and focused, making her more confident and articulate.

Then there's Peter, an athlete who swears by diaphragmatic breathing. He uses it to enhance his performance, saying it helps him stay centered and focused during competitions.

Daily Usage

Incorporating these exercises into your daily routine is easier than you think.

- Set aside a few minutes in the morning and evening for practice.

- Use these techniques during stressful moments, like before a big meeting or when stuck in traffic.

- The key is consistency. The more you practice, the more natural it will become, and the quicker you can calm your mind and body when you need it most.

Breathing exercises are a simple yet powerful tool for managing stress and anxiety. By learning to control your breath, you can take control of your mind and body, paving the way for a more peaceful and balanced life.

Discover the Power of Visualization

Imagine standing on a beach, the waves gently lapping at your feet, the sun warming your skin, and the salty breeze filling your lungs. This is the essence of visualization, a technique that uses mental imagery to transport you to a place of calm and clarity.

Visualization is about creating mental pictures to achieve a more relaxed mind. While guided imagery involves a more structured approach with someone leading you through the visual journey, visualization can be self-directed and tailored to your needs.

Benefits

The benefits of visualization are manifold.

- It reduces stress, improves focus, and enhances mental clarity.

- Athletes have used it for decades to enhance performance, mentally rehearsing their routines perfectly.

- Visualization can also be a powerful tool for managing overthinking. When your mind is stuck in a loop of worries and what-ifs, visualization can provide an escape route, redirecting your thoughts toward something positive and calming.

EXERCISES

4E. To get started with visualization, find a quiet, comfortable place where you won't be disturbed.

- Close your eyes and take a few deep breaths.

- Begin by imagining a peaceful place, like that beach we discussed earlier.

- Engage all your senses: feel the sun's warmth, hear the gentle waves, see the vibrant colors of the ocean, and smell the salty air.

- Spend a few minutes immersing yourself in this scene.

- This practice can help reduce stress and create a sense of tranquility.

4F. For goal-oriented visualization, picture yourself achieving a specific goal.

- If you have an upcoming presentation, imagine yourself standing confidently, speaking clearly, and receiving positive feedback from your audience.

- Visualize every detail, from the clothes you're wearing to the expressions on your listeners' faces.

- This mental rehearsal can boost your confidence and improve your performance.

4G. Guided imagery for relaxation is another effective technique.

- Imagine you're walking through a serene forest.

- Hear the birds chirping, feel the cool breeze, and see the sunlight filtering through the trees.

- Let yourself be fully present in this scene, allowing the peaceful imagery to wash away your stress.

- Guided imagery can be beneficial when you're overwhelmed, offering a mental oasis to recharge.

The science behind visualization is fascinating. When you visualize, you activate the visual cortex in your brain, the same area that processes actual visual information. This activation helps form new neural pathways, reinforcing positive behaviors and reducing stress. Visualization can also lower the fight-or-flight response, calming the body and mind.

Consider the story of Emma, a student preparing for her final exams. She used visualization to imagine herself confidently answering questions and acing her tests. This mental rehearsal reduced her anxiety and improved her focus, leading to better performance.

There's Francisco, a project manager who visualized the successful completion of a major project. He pictured every step in his mind, from initial planning to the final presentation. This mental imagery helped him stay organized, motivated, and ultimately successful.

Visualization is a powerful tool for managing overthinking, reducing stress, and achieving goals. By creating positive mental images, you can transform your thought patterns and cultivate a sense of calm and clarity. So, the next time your mind starts to spiral, close your eyes, take a deep breath, and let the power of visualization guide you to a place of peace.

Use Positive Affirmations Effectively

Definition: **Positive affirmations** are simple, positive statements you repeat to yourself to challenge and overcome self-sabotaging and negative thoughts.

Affirmations are like pep talks for your brain. They rewire your brain for positive thinking, helping you believe in the reality of what you're affirming to yourself. By consistently repeating these affirmations, you can change your mindset, build self-confidence, and reduce stress. Psychologically, affirmations can boost your mood, increase your self-worth, and enhance your overall mental well-being. They can be potent tools for fostering a positive outlook on life.

Creating effective affirmations is both an art and a science.

- First, use present tense and positive language. Instead of saying, "I will be confident," say, "I am confident." This makes the affirmation feel more immediate and real.

- Focus on specific goals and desires that are believable. If your affirmation is too far-fetched, your brain will reject it. Suppose you aim to boost your self-confidence. You might say, "I am confident and capable," or "I handle challenges gracefully."

- These statements are specific, positive, and achievable, making them more effective in rewiring your brain.

Daily Usage

Integrating affirmations into your daily life can amplify their impact.

- Start by repeating your affirmations during your morning routine. As you brush your teeth or make your coffee, say your affirmations out loud or in your head.

- Writing your affirmations in a journal can also be powerful. The act of writing helps reinforce the belief in your mind.

- You can also use affirmation apps or sticky notes to remind yourself throughout the day. Place sticky notes with affirmations on your bathroom mirror, computer monitor, or refrigerator.

- The consistency of regularly exposing yourself to these positive statements can make a significant difference.

Consider Sue, who struggled with self-doubt at work. She started using the affirmation, "I am confident in my abilities," every morning and wrote it in her journal each night. Over time, she noticed a shift in her mindset. She became more assertive in meetings and confidently took on new challenges.

Then there's José, who used affirmations to improve his work performance. His affirmation, "I am focused and productive," helped him stay on track during busy days. He placed sticky notes around his workspace and repeated the affirmation whenever he felt overwhelmed. The result? Improved productivity and a sense of accomplishment.

Affirmations can be a game-changer in your mental well-being toolkit. They are simple yet powerful statements that can help you overcome negative thoughts and build a positive mindset. By creating personalized affirmations and integrating them into your daily routine, you can see real changes in your outlook and confidence. Whether you say them aloud, write them down, or use visual reminders, consistently practicing positive affirmations can help you rewire your brain and foster a more positive, resilient mindset.

Defuse the Unexpected with Quick Stress-Relief Techniques

Imagine you're in the middle of a hectic day, juggling multiple tasks, and suddenly, your boss drops an urgent project on your desk. Your mind races, and your stress levels skyrocket. This is where quick stress-relief techniques come into play.

Immediate intervention is crucial to prevent stress from spiraling out of control and escalating into full-blown anxiety. These quick techniques are your go-to tools when you need to calm down fast, whether in a meeting, stuck in traffic, or feeling overwhelmed.

One effective method is **progressive muscle relaxation**. This involves tensing then slowly releasing different muscle groups in your body, helping to alleviate physical tension and promote relaxation.

- Start by sitting comfortably and taking a few deep breaths.

- Begin with your toes, clenching them tightly for a few seconds before releasing.

- Gradually move up through your body—calves, thighs, abdomen, arms, and face.

- This technique helps you become more aware of physical sensations, making it easier to release stress.

Another quick and powerful technique is the **5-4-3-2-1 grounding exercise**. Engaging your senses helps bring your focus back to the present moment. This sensory exercise can quickly divert your mind from stress and anxiety, grounding you in the present.

- Start by identifying **five** things you can see,

- **four** things you can touch,

- **three** things you can hear,

- **two** things you can smell and

- **one** thing you can taste.

Quick stretching exercises can also be very beneficial. These simple movements can help release physical tension and improve blood flow, making you feel more relaxed and energized.

- Stand up, stretch your arms above your head, and take a deep breath.

- Reach down to touch your toes, feeling your back and legs stretch.

- Rotate your neck gently from side to side, releasing any tension.

Aromatherapy with essential oils is another effective quick fix. Essential oils can stimulate your brain's limbic system, which controls emotions and memory, promoting a sense of calm and well-being.

- Keep a small bottle of lavender or peppermint oil at your desk.

- When stress hits, take a moment to inhale the soothing scent deeply.

Tapping, or Emotional Freedom Techniques (EFT), is a stress-reduction method that combines physical touch with verbal affirmations.

- Tap gently on specific points on your body, like the side of your hand, eyebrows, or nose, while repeating positive phrases like, "I am calm and in control."

- This technique can help disrupt negative thought patterns and promote emotional balance.

Visualization of a safe space can also be incredibly calming.

- Close your eyes and imagine a place where you feel completely safe and relaxed. It could be a beach, a forest, or a cozy room.

- Engage all your senses to see the colors, hear the sounds, and feel the textures.

- This mental escape can provide a quick respite from stress and anxiety.

The science behind these quick stress-relief techniques is compelling. They activate the parasympathetic nervous system, which counteracts the stress response. This leads to an immediate reduction in cortisol levels, the hormone responsible for stress. By calming the nervous system, these techniques can help you regain control and maintain focus.

Daily Usage

Incorporating these techniques into your daily routine is simple. Keep essential oils at your desk for easy access. Set reminders to take quick stretching breaks throughout the day. While these methods are highly effective, it's important to recognize their limitations. They are best used as immediate interventions and complement long-term stress management strategies.

Quick stress-relief techniques are invaluable tools for managing overthinking and reducing daily stress. They offer immediate relief, helping you stay calm and focused.

Create a Personal Stress Management Plan

Do you ever feel like stress is a constant, unwelcome guest that won't leave? That's where a personal stress management plan comes in. It's your customized tool to fix life's hurdles without losing your cool. Think of it as a toolkit tailored to your unique needs and preferences.

A structured approach to managing stress can make all the difference. It helps you identify what triggers your stress and equips you with effective strategies to handle it. Having a plan means you're not caught off guard when stress strikes; you're prepared and proactive.

Exercises

4H. Creating your stress management plan starts with assessing your current stress levels and triggers.

- Take a moment to jot down what typically stresses you out. Is it work deadlines, family obligations, or social situations? Understanding what sets you off is the first step to managing it.

- Next, identify effective stress-relief techniques that work for you. It could be a quick walk, listening to your favorite music, or practicing deep breathing. The key is to find activities that genuinely help you relax and recharge.

- Setting realistic and achievable goals is crucial. Start small and build from there. If you want to practice mindfulness daily, begin with just five minutes and gradually increase the time. The idea is to set yourself up for success, not overwhelm.

Use practical tools to help you design and implement your plan.

4I. Take the following stress assessment quiz to understand your stress levels clearly.

Stress Self-Assessment Quiz

Use the scale below to rate how often each statement applies to you:
Hardly Ever – 1
Not Often – 2
Sometimes – 3
Frequently – 4
Almost Always – 5

1. _____ I feel overwhelmed by the demands of work, family, or personal responsibilities.

2. _____ I have difficulty relaxing, even during leisure time or when I have nothing urgent to do.

3. _____ I am irritable or easily frustrated with others, even over small things.

4. _____ I often have trouble concentrating or staying focused on tasks.

5. _____ I feel physically tense, with tight muscles, headaches, or jaw clenching.

6. _____ I experience difficulty falling asleep or staying asleep due to racing thoughts.

7. _____ I worry frequently about things that are beyond my control.

8. _____ I feel tired or exhausted, even after what should be a restful night of sleep.

9. _____ I struggle to find time for self-care, hobbies, or enjoyable activities.

10. _____ I'm constantly in "fight or flight" mode, always ready for something to go wrong.

_____ Calculate Your Total Score

Scoring

10–19: Low Level of Stress

- **Evaluation**: You experience minimal stress, which generally doesn't interfere with your daily life.

- **Recommended Action**: Continue practicing healthy habits like regular exercise, adequate sleep, and mindfulness techniques to maintain balance and prevent stress from escalating. Engage in stress-prevention activities such as socializing and maintaining a balanced routine to stay resilient against future stressors.

20–29: Moderate Level of Stress

- **Evaluation**: You experience stress regularly, which can cause occasional disruptions in your mood or productivity.

- **Recommended Action**: Develop a routine for relaxation and self-care, such as setting aside time each day to unwind. Incorporate stress-management practices like deep breathing exercises, physical activity, and time management techniques. Consider delegating tasks and adjusting your workload to reduce your daily stress load.

30–39: High Level of Stress

- **Evaluation**: Stress is frequently present in your life and likely impacts your mental and physical health.

- **Recommended Action**: Focus on reducing stress by identifying its primary sources and taking proactive steps to manage them. This could involve delegating tasks, reassessing your workload, or seeking help from a therapist. Use stress-relief techniques such as mindfulness meditation, yoga, or progressive muscle relaxation. Prioritize self-care and work on restoring balance in your life.

40–50: Severe Level of Stress

- **Evaluation**: Stress has become overwhelming and is significantly affecting your well-being. You may feel chronically exhausted, irritable, or physically unwell.

- **Recommended Action**: It's essential to seek professional help to manage your stress, such as therapy or stress-management coaching. In the meantime, reduce your stress by learning to say no, prioritizing self-care, and practicing relaxation techniques like yoga, biofeedback, or journaling. Building a support network can also relieve some of your burdens.

Exercises

4J. Worksheets to build a stress reduction plan help you outline your objectives and the steps needed to achieve them. The 6 sample Stress Reduction Plan worksheets on the following pages each correspond with the numbered steps below.

Tips for Success

- **Start small**: Don't overwhelm yourself by setting too many goals simultaneously.

- **Be flexible**: Adjust your goals or timeline if you encounter challenges.

- **Celebrate progress**: Acknowledge and reward yourself for reaching milestones.

- **Stay committed**: Stress reduction is a long-term effort, so stick with your plan and reassess regularly.

Stress Reduction Plan

1. **Identify Your Stressors:** List the primary sources of stress in your life and how each affects you. Be as specific as possible. For example: "Work deadlines," "Financial pressure," "Family responsibilities," "Health concerns," etc.

2. **Set Goals & Actionable Steps:** Write down clear, specific goals that focus on managing or reducing your identified stressors, and identify why each goal is important to you. For each goal, break it into small, manageable steps. This will help make the process less overwhelming and more achievable. For example, the steps for "Reduce work-related stress" could be one of these.
   - Create a daily to-do list.
   - Prioritize tasks by importance.
   - Delegate tasks when possible.

3. **Set a Timeline for Each Goal:** Create a timeline to track your progress and stay motivated. Be realistic about when you want to achieve each goal. For example, "Complete budgeting plan within two weeks" or "Start a daily mindfulness routine within the next month."

4. **Identify Potential Challenges:** Write down obstacles or challenges that might prevent you from reaching your goals. Then, brainstorm solutions to overcome these obstacles. For example, "Challenge: I struggle to make time for relaxation. Solution: Schedule 10 minutes for relaxation each morning."

5. **Track Your Weekly Progress:** Write down your progress weekly, noting how well you're implementing your action steps and what you might need to adjust.

6. **Review and Reflect:** At the end of your timeline, review how well you met your goals. Reflect on what worked and didn't and how you can continue managing stress moving forward.

Stress Reduction Goals – Identify Your Stressors
WORKSHEET 1 ©

List the primary sources of stress in your life and how each affects you. Be as specific as possible.

- **Example:** "Work deadlines," "Financial pressure," "Family responsibilities," "Health concerns," etc.

Primary Stressors	How It Affects Me

Stress Reduction Goals – Set Goals & Action Steps
WORKSHEET 2 ©

Write down specific goals that focus on managing or reducing your identified stressors. Identify why each goal is important to you.

Break each goal into small, manageable steps. This will help make the process less overwhelming and more achievable.

Goal	Why This Goal is Important to Me	Action Steps

Stress Reduction Goals – Timeline
Worksheet 3 ©

Create a timeline to track your progress and stay motivated. Include a target completion date and milestones along the way. Be realistic about when you want to achieve each goal.

Goal	Target Date	Milestones

Stress Reduction Goals – Potential Challenges
WORKSHEET 4 ©

Think about obstacles or challenges that might prevent you from reaching your goals and write them down. Then, brainstorm solutions to overcome these obstacles.

Goal	Potential Challenges	Possible Solution

Stress Reduction Goals – Weekly Progress
Worksheet 5 ©

Write down your progress weekly, noting how well you're implementing your action steps and what you might need to adjust.

Goal	Date	Progress Notes	Adjustments Needed

Stress Reduction Goals – Review & Reflect
WORKSHEET 6 ©

At the end of your timeline, review how well you met your goals. Reflect on what worked and didn't and how you can continue managing stress moving forward.

Goal	What Worked Well	What Needs Improvement	Next Steps

Exercises

4K. Use Daily or weekly planners for your stress management plan to keep you on track and ensure you're dedicating time to stress-relief activities.

4L. Regularly review and adjust your plan for long-term success. Life is dynamic, and so are your stressors.

- Periodically evaluate your plan to see what's working and what's not.

- Track your progress to detect valuable insights and highlight areas for improvement.

- Reflect on the most effective techniques and consider integrating new strategies if needed.

- Stay flexible and open to new approaches to keep your stress management plan relevant and effective.

Think about Leesa, who created her stress management plan after feeling overwhelmed by her job. She started by identifying her triggers: tight deadlines and lengthy meetings. She incorporated stress-relief techniques like quick walks during breaks and listening to calming music while working. Setting small, achievable goals helped her stay consistent. She used stress assessment questionnaires and goal-setting worksheets to track her progress. Regular reviews allowed her to adjust her plan, ensuring it remained effective. As a result, Leesa felt more in control and less stressed, improving her work performance and overall well-being.

Creating a personal stress management plan empowers you to take control of your stress rather than letting it control you. By understanding your triggers, setting realistic goals, and regularly reviewing your plan, you can manage stress more effectively and enjoy a more balanced life.

Next, we'll explore how to boost self-confidence and self-compassion further to enhance your mental well-being.

CHAPTER 5

ENHANCE SELF-CONFIDENCE WITH SELF-COMPASSION

Imagine that you're getting ready for a big presentation at work. You've practiced your slides and rehearsed your speech, but that familiar voice creeps in as you look in the mirror. "You're going to mess this up. Everyone will see you're a fraud." That's your inner critic, and it's time to show it the door.

Recognize Your Inner Critic

Definition: Your **inner critic** is an inner voice that criticizes your thoughts, behaviors, and emotions. This often leads to self-loathing, low self-esteem, and a persistent sense of inner doubt.

It's like an annoying friend who always points out your flaws but never offers solutions. This voice can be relentless, feeding into negative thought patterns that keep you in a cycle of overthinking and self-sabotage.

Definition: Self-talk is the ongoing dialogue you have with yourself throughout the day. It can be positive and uplifting or negative and destructive.

The inner critic falls into the latter category, perpetuating harmful inner dialogue that undermines confidence. While constructive self-criticism can help you grow by identifying areas for improvement, the inner critic is harsh and unforgiving, focusing solely on your perceived failures and shortcomings.

Common phrases associated with the inner critic include, "You're not good enough," "You always mess things up," and "Why can't you be like everyone else?" These thoughts are not only unhelpful but also damaging to your mental health.

Recognizing It

The inner critic typically manifests in a few recognizable ways.

- The harsh judgment of oneself is a hallmark of the inner critic, where every mistake is magnified, and every achievement is downplayed.

- Persistent feelings of inadequacy and self-doubt are common, making you question your abilities and worth.

- The inner critic loves to replay past mistakes and failures, reminding you of every misstep to keep you in perpetual regret and anxiety.

Its Origin

Where does this inner critic come from?

- It often has its roots in **early childhood experiences**. Suppose you grew up with critical parents or teachers. In that case, you might have internalized their negative feedback, transforming it into your inner voice.

- Societal and cultural expectations also play a role. We're constantly bombarded with messages about what we should look like, how we should act, and what we should achieve, creating unrealistic standards that fuel the inner critic.

Impacts

The impact of the inner critic on self-esteem is profound.

- This relentless negativity undermines your self-confidence, making you feel like you're never good enough.

- It creates a vicious cycle where self-doubt leads to more mistakes, which fuels further self-doubt.

- Over time, the inner critic perpetuates negative self-beliefs, making breaking free from its grip difficult.

Manage It

The good news is that you can manage and quiet your inner critic.

- Visualization exercises are a powerful tool. Imagine your inner critic as a cartoon villain. Visualize yourself shrinking it down to size or locking it in a box.

- Naming and externalizing the inner critic can also help. To distance yourself from its negativity, give it a ridiculous name, like "Naggy Nancy" or "Critical Carl."

- Self-dialogue techniques involve talking back to your inner critic. When it says, "You're going to fail," respond with, "Thanks for your input, but I've got this."

- Mindfulness exercises can help you observe your self-talk without judgment. When negative thoughts arise, acknowledge them and let them pass like clouds in the sky.

- Writing exercises are another practical method. Externalize your negative thoughts by writing them down. Then, challenge them by writing a more balanced perspective next to each one.

Get Rid of It

Self-compassion is the antidote to the inner critic.

- It involves treating yourself with the kindness and understanding you would offer a friend.

- Techniques for practicing self-compassion include loving-kindness meditation, where you focus on sending love and kindness to yourself.

- Self-compassionate self-talk involves replacing harsh criticisms with gentle encouragement.

- Writing a letter to yourself as you would to a friend in the same situation can also be incredibly healing.

The benefits of a kinder inner dialogue are immense. Self-compassion reduces self-criticism, increases emotional stability, and enhances overall well-being. It allows you to embrace your imperfections and see them as part of the human experience rather than as personal failings. So the next time your inner critic speaks up, remember: you can quiet it with self-compassion and reclaim your self-confidence.

Understand Your Emotional Triggers

Imagine you're in a conversation, and someone makes a casual comment about your work. Your heart races, your palms sweat, and suddenly, you're flooded with anxiety. These intense reactions are emotional triggers at play.

DEFINITION: Emotional triggers are situations or interactions that provoke strong emotional responses. They're those moments when something small sets off a cascade of feelings like criticism, rejection, and failure, each capable of turning your day upside down.

RECOGNIZING THEM

Recognizing your emotional triggers is crucial for managing them.

- Start by keeping an emotional trigger diary. Whenever you experience a strong emotional reaction, jot down what happened, how you felt, and what thoughts went through your mind.

- Reflective journaling prompts can help, too. Ask yourself questions like, "What situations make me feel most anxious?" or "When do I feel most criticized?"

- Over time, patterns will emerge, revealing your specific triggers. Identifying these can be eye-opening and empowering, giving you a clearer picture of what sets you off and why.

IMPACTS

The impact of emotional triggers on your behavior and relationships can be substantial.

- In the heat of the moment, you might react with anger, sadness, or anxiety, which can strain your interactions and cloud your judgment. For example, if criticism is a trigger, you might respond defensively, even to constructive feedback, creating tension in your relationships.

- Over time, these reactions can erode trust and intimacy, leading to long-term issues like chronic stress and emotional exhaustion.

- Emotional triggers can affect your well-being, making you feel like you're constantly on edge, waiting for the next emotional bomb to drop.

Consider Renae, a project manager who often felt overwhelmed by workplace criticism. By keeping an emotional trigger diary, she identified that her anxiety spiked during performance reviews. Recognizing this pattern, she worked on reframing her thoughts about feedback, viewing it as an opportunity for growth rather than a personal attack. This shift in perspective helped her manage her emotional responses better, improving her work relationships and overall confidence.

Another case is Paul, who struggled with feelings of rejection in his personal relationships. He realized that his anxiety often stemmed from past experiences of being excluded. By understanding this trigger, Paul began communicating more openly with his friends and partner about his feelings, reducing misunderstandings and strengthening his connections.

Identifying and managing emotional triggers isn't about avoiding difficult situations but about understanding your reactions and learning to navigate them more effectively. You can develop strategies to handle these moments more calmly and clearly by pinpointing what sets you off.

Use Techniques for Emotional Processing

Imagine you're carrying around a backpack filled with heavy, unprocessed emotions. Every time you face stress or anxiety, another brick gets added. Over time, this backpack weighs you down, making it harder to move forward.

Emotional processing is the act of taking out those bricks of unprocessed emotions, examining them, and finding a place to set them down. It's about dealing with your feelings in a healthy way rather than letting them accumulate and overwhelm you. When you process emotions effectively, you improve your mental and emotional health, reducing stress and increasing overall well-being.

Writing in an emotional journal is one of the most accessible emotional processing methods.

- Sit down with a notebook and pour your feelings onto the pages. Don't worry about grammar or coherence; just let your thoughts flow.

- Reflect on your writing and notice any patterns or recurring themes.

Art therapy is another powerful technique.

- Grab some colored pencils or paints and express your emotions visually.
- You don't need to be an artist; the act of creating is what's therapeutic.

Physical activities like running or dancing can also help release pent-up emotions.

- When your body moves, your mind can process feelings more freely.

Mindfulness plays a crucial role in emotional processing.

- Observe your emotions without judgment, allowing you to experience them fully without being overwhelmed.

Mindful breathing can ground you during emotional turbulence.

- When you feel intense emotions, take a moment to focus on your breath.
- Inhale deeply, hold for a few seconds, then exhale slowly.
- This simple act can bring you back to the present moment and give you the space to process your feelings.

Consider the story of Ana, who used art therapy to heal from a traumatic experience. She found that drawing her emotions allowed her to express feelings she couldn't put into words. Over time, her anxiety decreased, and she felt more at peace.

Then there's Wesley, who managed his emotional stress through physical activity. Whenever he felt overwhelmed, he'd go outside to run, letting the rhythm of his footsteps and the fresh air clear his mind. This practice helped him process his emotions and maintain emotional balance.

Processing your emotions isn't a one-time fix; it's an ongoing practice. You can keep your emotional backpack from getting too heavy by incorporating techniques like journaling, art therapy, physical activity, and mindfulness. Whether dealing with daily stressors or deeper emotional wounds, these methods can help you navigate your feelings and find a healthier, more balanced state of mind.

Build Resilience Through Self-Compassion

Imagine a friend coming to you after making a mistake, feeling down and defeated. You'd offer them words of comfort, emphasizing that everyone makes mistakes and they're still valuable and capable. Now, imagine offering that same kindness to yourself. That's the essence of self-compassion.

Definition: **Self-compassion** is treating yourself with the same understanding and patience you'd extend to a friend.

It consists of three components: self-kindness, common humanity, and mindfulness.

- **Self-kindness** means being gentle and supportive towards yourself, especially when you fail or make mistakes.

- **Common humanity** involves recognizing that everyone struggles and makes mistakes; you're not alone in your imperfections.

- **Mindfulness** is about being present with your emotions without getting swept away.

It's crucial to understand that self-compassion isn't self-pity. While self-pity means wallowing in your suffering, self-compassion is about acknowledging your pain but not letting it define you.

Exercises

To cultivate self-compassion, try some practical exercises.

5A. Loving-kindness meditation is a fantastic starting point.

- Sit comfortably, close your eyes, and focus on sending love and kindness first to yourself, then to others.

- Repeat phrases like, "May I be happy. May I be healthy. May I be safe."

5B. Techniques for self-compassionate self-talk are also helpful.

- When you catch yourself being self-critical, pause and reframe your thoughts.

- Instead of saying, "I'm such a failure," try, "I'm doing the best I can, and that's enough."

5C. Writing a letter to yourself is another powerful exercise.

- Imagine you're writing to a close friend who is going through a tough time.

- Offer the same support and encouragement you'd give them.

- This practice can help shift your perspective and foster a kinder inner dialogue.

Benefits

Self-compassion has profound benefits.

- It reduces self-criticism, which is often a significant source of stress and anxiety.

- Being kinder to yourself increases your emotional stability and resilience.

- You're better equipped to handle setbacks because you view them as part of the human experience rather than personal failures.

- This shift in mindset can significantly enhance your overall well-being.

- Research has shown that individuals who practice self-compassion have higher self-esteem, lower levels of depression and anxiety, and greater life satisfaction. It's a powerful tool for improving mental health and emotional resilience.

Consider the story of Penny, who struggled with self-criticism. She constantly felt inadequate and was her own worst enemy. By practicing self-compassion, Penny learned to offer herself the same kindness she gave to others. She started with loving-kindness meditation, which gradually helped her feel more connected and less isolated in her struggles. Over time, Penny noticed a significant decrease in her self-critical thoughts and an increase in her emotional well-being.

Another example is Terry, who used self-compassion to build resilience. Terry faced numerous setbacks in his career, and the constant pressure took a toll on his mental health. He began incorporating self-compassionate self-talk into his daily routine, reminding himself that everyone faces challenges and that it's okay to make mistakes. This practice helped Terry bounce back from setbacks more quickly and approach his work with renewed energy and confidence.

Adopt the Body Language of Confidence

Imagine walking into a room, shoulders slumped, eyes darting around nervously. Now, imagine walking in, standing tall, and making eye contact. The difference is palpable, right? That's the power of body language. It's not just about how others perceive you; it's also about how you perceive yourself.

When you adopt confident body language, you send signals to your brain that boost your self-esteem. It's the psychology of body language at work. Non-verbal cues like posture, eye contact, and gestures can significantly impact confidence. When you stand tall and make eye contact, you tell yourself and others, "I've got this."

So, how do you adopt confident body language?

- Start with your posture. Stand up straight, pull your shoulders back, and keep your head high. Think of how superheroes stand—channel that energy.

- Next, focus on making eye contact. It might feel uncomfortable initially, but looking someone in the eye about 60% of the time can make a huge difference. It shows you're engaged and confident.

- Use open and expansive gestures. Avoid crossing your arms or hunching over; these are defensive postures. Instead, use your hands to emphasize points when you speak and take up space. It's like saying, "I belong here."

Body language doesn't just influence how you feel about yourself; it also affects how others perceive you.

- Confident body language can build trust and rapport, making your interactions smoother and more effective.

- People are more likely to trust and take you seriously when you project confidence. This is especially important in professional settings. Imagine giving a presentation with a confident stance and clear eye contact. Your audience is more likely to be engaged and receptive to your message.

- Confident body language also enhances effective communication. It's easier to get your point across when you're not fidgeting or looking away.

Exercises

Try some practical exercises to practice and refine your body language.

5D. Start with mirror exercises.

- Stand in front of a mirror and observe your posture and gestures.
- Make adjustments as needed and practice until it feels natural.

5E. Role-playing scenarios can also be helpful.

- Practice with a friend or family member, taking turns being the speaker and the listener.
- Focus on maintaining confident body language throughout the interaction.

5F. Daily practice routines are essential.

- Set aside a few minutes daily to practice standing tall, making eye contact, and using open gestures. Over time, these habits will become second nature.

Imagine Pat, who used to struggle with public speaking. Pat practiced confident body language daily, using mirror exercises and role-playing with a friend. Over time, Pat's confidence grew, and she was not just surviving presentations but excelling in them.

Or think of Trevor, who used confident body language to build better relationships at work. By making eye contact and using open gestures, he gained the trust of his colleagues and improved his communication skills. These small changes in body language can profoundly impact your confidence and interactions.

Manage Emotional Reactions in Real-Time

Imagine you're in a tense conversation and feel your blood pressure rising. Your heart starts to race, and you can feel anger bubbling up. This is where real-time emotion management becomes crucial.

Managing emotions as they arise can prevent minor issues from escalating into full-blown conflicts. It helps you maintain control, think clearly, and respond appropriately. Immediate emotional regulation strategies are helpful and necessary for personal and professional interactions. They can help you stay composed during a heated argument, keep calm in a stressful meeting, or navigate daily frustrations more smoothly.

One effective technique for managing emotions in the moment is **the STOP technique**. This stands for **S**top, **T**ake a breath, **O**bserve, and **P**roceed.

- When you feel overwhelmed, literally tell yourself to "**Stop**."
- **Take** a deep breath to calm your nervous system.
- **Observ**e what's happening inside and around you, and acknowledge your feelings without judgment.
- **Proceed** with a more composed and thoughtful response.

Another simple yet powerful method is **the 10-second rule**.

- When you feel an immediate emotional reaction, pause for ten seconds before responding.

- This brief pause lets you collect your thoughts and choose a more measured response.

Grounding techniques can also be incredibly effective.

- These involve focusing on your senses to anchor yourself in the present moment.

- For example, you might focus on the feeling of your feet on the ground, the sounds around you, or the texture of an object in your hand.

BENEFITS

- Managing emotions in real-time can significantly improve relationships and decision-making abilities. When you handle your emotions well, you reduce the risk of conflicts and improve communication. People are more likely to respond positively when you're calm and composed.

- Another benefit is enhanced decision-making under pressure. Staying grounded allows you to think more clearly and make better choices, even in stressful situations. This improves your interactions with others and boosts your self-confidence and overall mental well-being.

Let's talk about practical examples.

Imagine you're in a heated argument with a close friend. You feel your anger rising but decide to use the STOP technique. You tell yourself to stop, take a deep breath, and observe your feelings. You realize that your anger is more about feeling unappreciated than the actual topic of the argument. With this insight, you explain your feelings calmly, leading to a more constructive conversation.

Or consider a stressful work meeting where tensions are high. You feel the urge to snap back at a colleague's criticism. Instead, you apply the 10-second rule. You pause, take a deep breath, and then respond with a composed and thoughtful remark. This defuses the tension and demonstrates your ability to stay calm under pressure.

Real-time emotion management is like having a superpower. It allows you to navigate life's challenges with grace and resilience, improving your relationships and decision-making. By mastering these techniques, you can turn emotionally charged situations into opportunities for growth and connection.

Enhance Empathy for Understanding in Relationships

Imagine a friend confiding in you about a tough day. You listen attentively, nod, and maybe even feel their frustration or sadness as if it were your own. This ability to understand and share the feelings of another person is empathy.

Empathy is a powerful tool in building and maintaining personal and professional relationships. It comes in three flavors: cognitive, emotional, and compassionate.

- Cognitive empathy is about understanding someone else's perspective.

- Emotional empathy involves feeling what another person is experiencing.

- Compassionate empathy goes a step further by not only understanding and feeling but also being moved to help.

Developing empathy isn't just about being a good listener; it's about truly connecting with others on a deeper level.

- Start with **active listening**. When someone is speaking, focus entirely on them. Don't just hear their words; listen to their emotions and observe their body language. Avoid interrupting; instead, reflect on what you've heard to show you understand.

- Aim for **perspective-taking**. Try to put yourself in the other person's shoes, imagining how they feel in their situation. This can be as simple as thinking, "What would I feel if I were in their position?"

- Ask **open-ended questions**. Instead of asking yes/no questions, ask questions that encourage the other person to share more, like "How did that make you feel?" or "What do you think will happen next?"

Benefits

Empathy strengthens connections and builds trust.

- When people feel understood, they're more likely to open up and share their true selves, leading to deeper, more meaningful relationships.
- This reduces misunderstandings and conflicts because you're not just hearing but understanding where the other person is coming from.
- In professional settings, empathy fosters better teamwork and collaboration. When team members feel their perspectives are valued, they're more engaged and motivated.

Consider the story of Laura, who improved her family dynamics through active listening. She used to interrupt her teenage daughter, thinking she knew what her daughter would say. When Laura started practicing active listening, she noticed a change. Her daughter felt heard and valued, and their relationship improved significantly.

Another example is Ted, a shipping manager who enhanced his team's performance by incorporating perspective-taking exercises. He encouraged his team to share their viewpoints openly and made a genuine effort to understand them, leading to better teamwork and less conflict.

Empathy is a skill that can be cultivated with practice. By consciously listening actively, taking others' perspectives, and asking open-ended questions, you can enhance your empathy and improve your relationships. It's about being present, showing genuine interest, and connecting on a human level.

Publisher's Note

For more about empathy, see Delia Sike's companion book, ***Empathy Unlocked—Learning to Connect in a Disconnected World.***

* Help Us Silence the Saboteur *

> The greatest weapon against stress is our ability to choose one thought over another.
>
> William James

Did you know overthinking can be a silent saboteur of happiness and mental clarity? By recognizing and breaking free from it, you're already taking steps toward a more peaceful mind—and we're so grateful you're on this journey with us.

Here's something to consider: Would you help someone struggling with overthinking, even if you didn't know them personally? Imagine that person for a moment. They could be trapped in a cycle of analysis paralysis, unsure how to move forward.

We aim to help as many people as possible silence the inner critic that fuels overthinking. But we can't do it alone. We need your help to spread the word and inspire others to take back control of their thoughts.

Your voice matters. Many people rely on reviews when deciding whether to pick up a book, so I'm asking you to leave a review for "Overthinking – The Silent Saboteur." A review is a small act that takes less than a minute but can make a big difference in someone else's life.

Your review could:

- Help one more person recognize their overthinking patterns.

- Help one more individual break free from analysis paralysis.

- Help one more reader sleep more soundly at night without mental chatter.

- Help one more professional find clarity in their decision-making.

- Help one more relationship thrive without the barriers of over-analysis.

Ready to help someone else silence their overthinking? It's easy! Just go to this book on Goodreads or on the website for the company from which you purchased the book, and leave your review with a rating, a video or photo, and your thoughts.

If "Overthinking -The Silent Saboteur" has helped you, consider passing it on to someone who could benefit from it.

With gratitude,
Delia Sikes

CHAPTER 6

REDUCE NIGHTTIME OVERTHINKING AND IMPROVE SLEEP

I magine it's 2 a.m., and you're wide awake, replaying that awkward encounter from three years ago when you accidentally called your boss "Mom." Your mind is like a late-night TV marathon, and you're stuck watching the worst episodes on repeat. Overthinking has hijacked your sleep, and you're desperate for a way to hit the off button.

If this sounds all too familiar, you're not alone. Overthinking at night is a common struggle that can wreak havoc on your sleep and overall well-being. So, let's uncover the science behind it and find ways to get you back to dreamland.

Understand the Science of Sleep and Overthinking

First, let's dive into how overthinking messes with your sleep.

- When your mind is racing with endless thoughts, it triggers nighttime anxiety.

- This anxiety acts like a noisy neighbor blasting music when you're trying to sleep. It keeps you awake, tossing and turning.

- Overthinking also disrupts sleep cycles. Usually, your brain transitions smoothly through different stages of sleep. But when you're anxious, it's like trying to drive on a road filled with potholes: bumpy and uncomfortable.

- This disruption mainly affects REM sleep, crucial for memory processing and emotional regulation.

Sleep isn't just one prolonged, continuous state. It's a series of stages, each with its own role.

- REM sleep is the stage where you dream, and it's vital for consolidating memories and processing emotions. When overthinking hijacks your night, it often cuts into your REM sleep, leaving you feeling foggy and emotionally off-kilter the next day.

- Then there's deep sleep, also known as slow-wave sleep. This stage is about physical restoration: repairing muscles, strengthening the immune system, and releasing growth hormones. Overthinking can make it hard to reach this stage, depriving your body of the rest it needs.

- Light sleep is the transitional stage, where your body prepares for deep sleep. An anxious mind can keep you in light sleep, preventing you from getting the restorative rest you need.

Overthinking increases cortisol levels, the body's primary stress hormone.

- Elevated cortisol acts like a double shot of espresso, making it hard to fall and stay asleep. It keeps your brain on high alert, making it challenging to transition into deep sleep.

- When anxiety is high, your brain struggles to shut down, and you end up in a state of hyperarousal.

- This constant alertness can make drifting off into a peaceful slumber nearly impossible.

Lack of sleep is a vicious cycle.

- The less you sleep, the more you overthink, and the more you overthink, the less you sleep.

- Sleep deprivation cranks up your stress levels, making you more susceptible to anxiety and depression.

- Your cognitive function also suffers. Simple tasks like remembering where you left your keys or focusing in a meeting become Herculean challenges.

- Chronic sleep deprivation can elevate your risk of developing anxiety disorders and depression, creating a downward spiral that's hard to escape.

Research backs up these connections. Studies on sleep patterns in individuals with anxiety show that they often experience fragmented sleep and spend less time in restorative stages. Insomnia is frequently linked with high levels of rumination, where the mind gets stuck in a loop of negative thoughts.

Research also shows poor sleep impairs decision-making, making it harder to think clearly and increasing the likelihood of overthinking.

For example, a study from **UC Berkeley** found that a sleepless night could trigger up to a 30% rise in anxiety levels. Deep sleep, particularly non-REM slow-wave sleep, calms and resets the anxious brain.

Another study published in the journal ***Nature Human Behaviour*** showed that insufficient sleep amplifies anxiety, while deep sleep reduces it. Functional MRI and polysomnography experiments revealed that after sleepless nights, the medial prefrontal cortex shuts down, and deeper emotional centers become overactive. Deep sleep restored the brain's prefrontal mechanism, reducing emotional reactivity.

Understanding the science behind sleep and overthinking is the first step to breaking this cycle. By recognizing how your mind and body interact, you can start to make changes that promote better sleep and reduce nighttime anxiety. The goal is to create a peaceful environment in your mind, allowing you to transition smoothly through the stages of sleep and wake up refreshed.

Prepare for Sleep with a Routine

Ever heard the term "sleep hygiene"? No, it's not about ensuring your bed is germ-free, although clean sheets feel amazing. Sleep hygiene refers to practices and habits that help you get a good night's sleep. It's like a bedtime ritual for grown-ups to ensure you fall asleep quickly and stay asleep through the night. Good sleep hygiene can improve mental and physical health, boost mood, and increase overall quality of life.

Let's talk about technology. Those glowing screens we're all addicted to are culprits in our sleep struggles. **Blue light** from phones, tablets, and computers messes with melatonin production, the hormone that regulates sleep. Your brain thinks blue light means daytime, delaying melatonin release and keeping you awake longer. The solution? Set screen time limits before bed. Try putting your devices away for at least an hour before you hit the pillow. Instead, pick up a book or listen to calming music.

Creating a pre-sleep routine can work wonders. Think of it as winding down, like a plane descending gently before landing.

- Start with activities that relax you: take a warm bath, do gentle stretches, or practice deep breathing exercises. Keep this routine consistent so your body knows it's time to sleep.

- Avoid heavy meals and alcohol right before bed. Your digestive system shouldn't be pulling an all-nighter.

- Caffeine is a sneaky sleep thief. Limit your caffeine intake to the mornings and early afternoons.

- A consistent sleep schedule is like setting your internal clock to the right time. Go to bed and wake up at consistent times every day, even on weekends. It might seem tedious, but your body will thank you.

Exercises

6A. Try these helpful tips to prepare for a refreshing night's sleep.

- **Limit screen time before bed:** Put devices away at least an hour before sleep.

- **Set up a relaxing pre-sleep routine**, such as a warm bath, gentle stretches, or deep breathing exercises.

- **Limit caffeine and alcohol intake:** Avoid these in the hours before bedtime.

- **Observe a consistent sleep schedule:** Go to bed and wake up at consistent times every day.

These steps might sound simple, but they can profoundly impact your sleep quality. It's all about creating a setting that signals to your body that it's time to shut down and rest. So, start incorporating these practices into your nightly routine and see how they transform your sleep. You deserve to wake up feeling refreshed and ready to tackle the day, not groggy and dreading the morning.

Create a Conducive Sleep Environment

Imagine your bedroom as a sanctuary. The physical environment where you sleep plays a crucial role in determining how well you rest. Falling asleep can feel like an uphill battle if your bed is uncomfortable or your room is too hot, bright, or noisy.

Start with **your bed.** Don't suffer like *The Princess and the Pea*, with discomfort keeping you awake all night. Choose a mattress supporting your body and pillows that align your neck. Comfortable bedding and pillows are more than just a luxury; they're necessary. Soft, breathable sheets can significantly affect how comfortable you feel.

The **temperature** of your bedroom should be like Goldilocks' porridge; —it needs to be just right. Experts recommend keeping the room cool, ideally between 60° — 67°F or 15.5° — 19.5°C. This temperature range helps your body's core temperature drop, signaling it's time to sleep. When it's too hot or cold, your body struggles to find that sweet spot, making it hard to drift off.

Darkness is another key player in the sleep game. Light exposure influences your body's production of melatonin, the sleep hormone. The darker your room, the better your body can produce melatonin, helping you fall and stay asleep.

- Blackout curtains can be a game-changer. They block out all external light, creating a pitch-dark environment perfect for sleep.

- Interior lights should be eliminated, whether from the glow of electronics or your alarm clock. If you need a night light for safety, use one that's motion-activated rather than always on.

Noise is another factor that can disrupt sleep. Whether it's a snoring partner, street noise, or a creaky house, unwanted sounds can keep you tossing and turning. White noise machines or earplugs can help mask these disruptions, providing a steady, soothing sound that lulls you to sleep.

Exercises

6B. Optimize your sleep environment with the following changes to improve your sleep quality.

- Does your mattress support your body? Does your pillow align with your neck? If not, then replace them. They're an investment in your physical and mental health.

- Make sure your sheets are soft and breathable. This can significantly affect whether you feel comfortable.

- Keep your room cool, aiming for a temperature range of 60°—67°F or 15.5°—19.5°C.

- Does exterior light shine into your room? Invest in curtains with a blackout lining or blackout shades to block intrusive light.

- Is there interior light invading your sleep haven?

    - Close the door to block light from another room.

    - Put a piece of tape or cloth over the power-glow of electronics.

    - Dim your alarm clock and turn it away from the bed.

    - Replace an always-on nightlight with one that's motion-activated.

    - Or consider wearing an eye mask.

- If noise is an issue, consider investing in a white noise machine or high-quality earplugs.

Decor also plays a role in setting the mood for sleep.

- Calming colors like blues and greens can create a serene atmosphere. These colors have a soothing effect on the mind, helping you relax and unwind.

- A minimalist bedroom design without clutter can reduce stress. When your room is tidy and organized, it's easier to feel calm and relaxed.

- Incorporating plants can improve air quality and promote a sense of well-being. Plants like lavender and jasmine purify the air and have calming scents that can enhance your sleep environment.

Take Rita, who struggled with insomnia for years, often waking up multiple times a night. After reading about the benefits of blackout curtains, she decided to try them. The difference was immediate; Rita slept through the night for the first time in years.

Consider Ian, who lived in a noisy urban area. The constant sound of traffic and late-night revelers kept him awake. He invested in a white noise machine, and it was a game-changer. The steady hum masked the disruptive sounds, allowing him to fall and stay asleep more easily.

Optimizing your sleep environment is about making small, thoughtful changes that can significantly impact your rest. Every detail counts, from the temperature of your room to the colors on your walls. Creating a sleep-friendly environment sets the stage for a restful night, helping you wake up refreshed and ready to tackle the day.

Adopt Relaxation Techniques for Better Sleep

Imagine lying in bed, staring at the ceiling, your mind racing like a hamster on a wheel. We've all been there. Relaxation techniques can be your secret weapon against this mental chaos. They help calm your mind and body, making it easier to fall asleep and stay asleep. Relaxation isn't just a luxury; it's a necessity for good mental and physical health. When you relax, you lower your stress levels, which can help you sleep better. Relaxation helps your body transition into sleep mode, reducing the time it takes to fall asleep and improving the quality of your rest.

Let's talk about some **relaxation techniques** that can make a real difference.

- Progressive muscle relaxation is a great place to start. This technique involves tensing and slowly releasing different muscle groups in your body. Start with your toes and work your way up to your head. Tighten each muscle group for about five seconds, then slowly release. The goal is to release physical tension, which can also help your mind relax.

- Another effective method is deep breathing exercises. Sit or lie comfortably, close your eyes, and take a deep breath through your nose, letting your abdomen expand. Hold your breath for a few seconds, then exhale slowly through your mouth. Repeat this process several times. Deep breathing helps activate your parasympathetic nervous system, which promotes relaxation.

- Visualization and guided imagery can also be incredibly soothing. Close your eyes and imagine a peaceful scene: a beach, a forest, or any place where you feel calm and safe. Engage all your senses: hear the waves crashing, feel the sand between your toes, smell the salty air.

- Guided imagery recordings can walk you through this process, making immersing yourself fully in the experience easier. These techniques create a mental escape, helping you distance yourself from stressful thoughts and focus on something calming.

The science behind relaxation techniques is fascinating. When you practice these methods, you reduce cortisol levels in your body. Cortisol is the primary stress hormone; high levels can keep you wired and awake. Lowering cortisol helps your body relax, making it easier to fall asleep.

Relaxation techniques also activate the parasympathetic nervous system, the part of your nervous system responsible for "rest and digest" activities. This activation counteracts the "fight or flight" response, helping your body and mind wind down.

Consider the story of Mike, a cybersecurity investigator who struggled with insomnia for years. After reading about its benefits, Mike decided to try progressive muscle relaxation. He started practicing it every night before bed, and the results were remarkable. Within a few weeks, Mike found it easier to fall asleep and noticed a significant improvement in his sleep quality.

Take Lena, a nurse who used guided imagery to manage her nighttime anxiety. She downloaded a guided imagery app and listened to it every night. The calming imagery helped her escape her racing thoughts, allowing her to drift off to sleep peacefully.

Relaxation techniques can be a game-changer for improving sleep. They offer a simple yet effective way to calm your mind and body, making it easier to transition into sleep mode. Incorporating these methods into your nightly routine can create a more peaceful and restful sleep environment. So, try one of these techniques next time you lie in bed and stare at the ceiling. You might be surprised at how they help you achieve a good night's sleep.

Use Guided Meditation for Nighttime Calm

Imagine lying in bed with your mind buzzing like a hive of bees, each thought louder and more urgent than the last. Guided meditation can be the soothing antidote to this chaos, helping to calm your mind before sleep. Meditation provides a structured focus, distracting your runaway thoughts and guiding you toward relaxation. Guided meditation enhances relaxation by calming your mind. It facilitates sleep onset, helping you drift off faster and enjoy deeper, more restorative sleep.

Let's walk through a few guided meditation scripts designed to bring you nighttime calm.

Exercises

6C. Try the body scan meditation for sleep.

- Begin by lying comfortably on your back.
- Close your eyes, take a deep breath, then slowly exhale.
- Start by focusing your attention on your toes and notice any sensations.
- Gradually move your focus up through your legs, torso, arms, and head.
- As you scan each part, consciously release any tension.
- This technique helps your body relax incrementally, making it easier to fall asleep.

6D. Try the loving-kindness meditation before bed.

- Sit or lie down comfortably.
- Close your eyes and take a few deep breaths.
- Start by directing kind and loving thoughts toward yourself. Silently repeat phrases like, "May I be happy. May I be healthy. May I be safe."

- After a few minutes, extend these wishes to someone you care about.

- Continue this process, expanding your circle to include friends, acquaintances, and even people you find challenging.

- This meditation fosters a sense of peace and emotional well-being, setting a tranquil tone for sleep.

6E. Try visualizing a serene landscape.

- Close your eyes and imagine a place where you feel completely relaxed. It could be a beach, a forest, or a meadow.

- Engage all your senses: hear the waves crashing, feel the soft sand under your feet, smell the salty air.

- This immersive experience helps shift your focus from anxious thoughts to a peaceful, calming scene, making it easier to fall asleep.

6F. Review these meditation apps, which can be a helpful tool in guiding you through these practices.

- **Headspace** offers a variety of sleep meditations, including guided breathing and sleepcasts (audio content designed to help a listener relax and prepare for sleep, combining elements of storytelling, soundscapes, and meditation techniques.)

- **Calm** provides soothing bedtime stories and soundscapes to lull you into sleep.

- **Insight Timer** boasts an extensive library of free guided meditations and music tracks specifically for sleep.

- These apps take the guesswork out of meditation, providing structured, easy-to-follow sessions to help you build consistent practice.

Consider Lynn, a busy professional in parts manufacturing who used to struggle with nighttime anxiety. She started using a body scan meditation from the **Calm** app. She followed the guided instructions each night before bed, focusing on relaxing her body one part at a time. Within a few weeks, Lynn found she was falling asleep more easily and staying asleep longer.

Think about Perry, who battled chronic stress and found solace in loving-kindness meditation. By incorporating this practice into his nightly routine, he gradually felt more at peace, improving his sleep quality significantly.

Guided meditation offers a powerful way to quiet your mind and prepare for a restful night. It provides a structured focus that helps you release anxious thoughts and embrace relaxation. Incorporating this practice into your bedtime routine can create a more peaceful and restorative sleep experience.

Real-Life Success Stories: From Insomnia to Restful Sleep

Imagine you're a professional who is juggling work deadlines, meetings, and a never-ending to-do list. You lie in bed at night, replaying the day's events and worrying about tomorrow. This was John's life.

John, an entertainment executive, was caught in a cycle of overthinking that left him tossing and turning every night. His constant stress at work only made things worse. He decided enough was enough. John started by creating a consistent bedtime routine. He set a specific bedtime, dimmed the lights an hour before, and turned off all electronic devices. He also transformed his bedroom into a sleep-friendly environment by keeping it cool, dark, and quiet.

John incorporated relaxation techniques like deep breathing and progressive muscle relaxation into his nightly routine. Within a few weeks, he noticed a significant improvement. John's sleep improved, and he woke refreshed and ready to tackle the day. John's performance soared, and he felt more confident and less stressed.

Then there's Natalya, a busy professional in higher education who struggled with racing thoughts every night. She turned to mindfulness meditation to quiet her mind. Natalya started with simple guided meditations before bed. She found a comfortable spot, closed her eyes, and followed the soothing voice guiding her through deep breaths and visualization exercises. This practice helped her shift her focus from anxious thoughts to calm.

Natalya also used body scan meditation, focusing on each part of her body, releasing tension and stress. These mindfulness practices became a nightly ritual, helping her transition smoothly into sleep. Natalya's anxiety levels dropped, and she experienced deeper, more restful sleep. Her overall well-being improved, and she felt more resilient to daily stressors.

The strategies and techniques used by John and Natalya are not only effective but also practical.

- Consistent bedtime routines signal to your body that it's time to wind down, making it easier to fall asleep.

- Creating a sleep-friendly environment eliminates distractions and promotes relaxation.

- Incorporating relaxation techniques like deep breathing and progressive muscle relaxation can help calm the mind and body, reducing stress and anxiety.

- Mindfulness practices, such as guided meditations, shift your focus away from racing thoughts, creating a mental space conducive to sleep.

Benefits

The outcomes and long-term benefits experienced by John and Natalya highlight the power of these techniques.

- Enhanced mental clarity and reduced overthinking are just the beginning.

- Improved mood and overall well-being follow, making daily challenges more manageable.

- Greater resilience to stress and anxiety means you're better equipped to handle whatever life throws your way.

- These positive changes create a ripple effect, improving your sleep and quality of life.

Action Items

So, what can you take away from these stories?

- First, consistency is key. Establish a bedtime routine and stick to it.

- Second, create a sleep-friendly environment. Keep your room cool, dark, and quiet.

- Third, incorporate relaxation techniques into your nightly routine. Try deep breathing, progressive muscle relaxation, or mindfulness meditation.

- Finally, be patient. Change takes time, but the results are worth it.

Remember, you can transform your sleep and improve your well-being. As the saying goes, "The best bridge between despair and hope is a good night's sleep."

The next chapter will explore overcoming professional self-sabotage and boosting your career success. You'll learn practical strategies to build confidence, manage stress, and achieve your professional goals.

CHAPTER 7

OVERCOME PROFESSIONAL SELF-SABOTAGE

I magine you're in a meeting, and your boss announces a new project that sounds perfect for you. Your heart races excitedly, but that familiar inner critic says, "You'll mess it up. Better let someone else take it." You sit quietly and watch the opportunity pass by. This is professional self-sabotage, plain and simple. It's like having a personal saboteur living rent-free in your head, constantly undermining your efforts and convincing you that you're not good enough.

RECOGNIZE PROFESSIONAL SELF-SABOTAGE

Professional self-sabotage manifests in various ways in the workplace.

- It's avoiding new projects because you're terrified of failing or, ironically, succeeding.

- It's missing deadlines because you're too busy perfecting every tiny detail.

- It's imposing limitations on yourself, convinced you're incapable or deserving of success.

These behaviors are often rooted in a fear of failure, which paralyzes you with the thought of making mistakes. They can also be rooted in a fear of success, which makes you worry about the increased expectations and responsibilities of success or feelings of imposter syndrome.

Common self-sabotage behaviors in professional settings are like old, worn-out habits that keep tripping you up.

- Over-preparation and perfectionism are the top culprits. You spend so much time ensuring everything is perfect that you never finish anything.

- Chronic lateness to meetings, whether physical or virtual, sends a message that you're unreliable, even if you're overthinking your presentation.

- Avoidance of networking opportunities is another big one. The thought of mingling with strangers makes you break out in a cold sweat, so you skip events that could advance your career.

Impacts

The impact of self-sabotage on your career growth is significant.

- Every missed opportunity for a promotion, every stunted professional relationship, is a victory for your inner saboteur.

- You watch colleagues move up the ladder while you remain stuck in the same position, frustrated and disheartened. It's like running on a treadmill while everyone else is sprinting ahead.

The psychological mechanisms behind this behavior are complex.

- Fear of failure keeps you from taking risks that could propel you forward.

- Fear of success makes you worry about the pressure of maintaining high standards.

- Impostor syndrome convinces you that you're a fraud and it's only a matter of time before everyone else figures it out.

- Low self-esteem whispers that you're not worthy of success, making you hesitate and doubt yourself at every turn.

Consider the story of Teresa, a customer care manager terrified of public speaking. She avoided presentations like the plague, convinced she'd embarrass herself. Her fear of failure was so intense that she'd find excuses to miss meetings or delegate her responsibilities to others. Her career stagnated until she decided enough was enough. She sought colleague feedback, practiced her presentations, and gradually built her confidence. Today, Teresa leads major projects and presents them easily, overcoming her fear through determination and support.

Another common example of workplace self-sabotage is missing deadlines. Take Tony, a software analyst who constantly procrastinated on his tasks. He'd start projects enthusiastically but overthink every detail, leading to missed deadlines and poor performance reviews. Realizing his pattern, Tony began setting realistic goals and seeking feedback from his team. He used cognitive reframing exercises to shift his mindset, viewing tasks as opportunities for growth rather than potential failures. Over time, Tony's productivity improved, and he regained his confidence.

Exercises

7A. To help you identify your self-sabotaging behaviors, answer the following self-sabotage identification checklist.

Self-Sabotage Identification Checklist

OVERTHINKING – THE SILENT SABOTEUR

Review each item on this checklist and mark those that apply frequently or intensely in your life. Recognizing these patterns is the first step toward addressing and overcoming self-sabotage.

1. Procrastination	___ Do you often delay starting tasks that you know are important? ___ Do you miss deadlines or complete tasks at the last minute under stress?
2. Negative Self-Talk	___ Do you frequently criticize yourself or doubt your abilities? ___ Do you often compare yourself unfavorably to others?
3. Overthinking	___ Do you spend excessive time thinking about past mistakes or worrying about future possibilities? ___ Do you obsess over details to the point where it prevents action?
4. Avoiding Challenges	___ Do you shy away from opportunities that might lead to personal growth due to fear of failure? ___ Do you avoid tasks or situations where you might not excel immediately?
5. Perfectionism	___ Do you have trouble completing tasks because they never feel good enough? ___ Do you set unrealistically high standards for yourself that are impossible to meet?
6. Self-Medicating	___ Do you frequently use alcohol, drugs, or other substances to cope with stress or emotional pain? ___ Do you use comfort-eating or other unhealthy habits to soothe yourself?
7. Relationship Sabotage	___ Do you create problems in good relationships without any real cause? ___ Do you have a pattern of ending relationships when they become too close or meaningful?
8. Financial Self-Sabotage	___ Do you spend money impulsively, incurring debt unnecessarily? ___ Do you avoid managing your finances or planning for financial security?
9. Neglecting Health	___ Do you often neglect exercise, diet, or medical advice, affecting your health adversely? ___ Do you prioritize other responsibilities over your well-being?
10. Resistance to Change	___ Do you resist or fear changes that could improve your life? ___ Do you cling to habits or people that hold you back from your potential?

7B. Reflect on recent professional setbacks and ask yourself if fear of failure or success played a role.

7C. Journaling can also be a powerful tool. Write about instances where you felt you held yourself back and explore the thoughts and emotions that accompanied those moments.

Once you've identified these behaviors, it's time to counteract them.

- Start by setting realistic goals and expectations.

- Break tasks into manageable steps and celebrate small victories along the way.

- Seek feedback and support from colleagues who can offer constructive criticism and encouragement.

- Cognitive reframing exercises can help you rewire your thought patterns. When negative thoughts arise, challenge them with positive affirmations and realistic assessments of your abilities.

Consider the story of Murali, a software engineer notorious for procrastination. Murali would put off tasks until the last minute, then scramble to complete them, often missing deadlines. Realizing this pattern, Murali began setting realistic goals and sought feedback from his team. He reframed his mindset, viewing each task as a step toward growth rather than a potential failure. Over time, his productivity soared, and his confidence returned.

Professional self-sabotage can be a formidable foe, but it can be overcome with self-awareness and proactive strategies. By recognizing and addressing these behaviors, you can unlock your full potential and achieve the career success you deserve.

Overcome Procrastination at Work

Imagine that you're staring at your to-do list, and instead of diving in, you find yourself scrolling through social media, organizing your desk, or even contemplating the meaning of life. Procrastination is that sneaky companion that convinces you to do anything but the task at hand.

Why do we procrastinate, especially at work?

- Often, it's rooted in a fear of failure. The thought of messing up can be so paralyzing that you'd rather not start at all.

- Task complexity can also contribute; when you're overwhelmed by the amount of work you have to do, it's easier to put it aside.

- Let's not forget perfectionism—that nagging need for everything to be flawless, which can lead to endless delays and second-guessing.

Procrastination and perfectionism are like two peas in a pod.

DEFINITION: Procrastination is putting off tasks despite knowing there will be negative consequences.

DEFINITION: Perfectionism is the relentless striving for flawlessness, accompanied by critical self-evaluations and concerns about others' evaluations.

When you combine the two, you get a toxic cocktail that leads to professional self-sabotage. The desire for everything to be perfect makes you hesitant to start, fearing you won't meet your own impossibly high standards. This hesitation becomes procrastination, creating a vicious cycle where nothing gets done.

IMPACTS

The impact of procrastination and perfectionism on your career can be devastating.

- Missed deadlines and opportunities become the norm, increasing stress and burnout.

- You're constantly trying to catch up, which affects your performance and reputation.

- The more you procrastinate, the more overwhelmed you become, and the harder it is to break free.

- A downward spiral leaves you feeling stuck and frustrated, watching colleagues move ahead while you're left behind.

So, how can you combat procrastination?

One effective technique is the **Pomodoro Technique**. This method involves setting a timer for 25 minutes and focusing solely on your task during that time. After the timer goes off, take a short break before starting another 25-minute session. This approach helps break tasks into manageable chunks, making them less overwhelming.

Time blocking is another strategy. Allocate specific time slots in your calendar for different tasks, ensuring you dedicate focused time to each one.

Breaking tasks into smaller steps makes them more approachable. Instead of thinking about the entire project, focus on the first step, then the next.

Setting deadlines and having **accountability partners** can help you stay on track. Share your goals with a colleague or friend who can monitor your progress and hold you accountable.

Exercises

7D. Here's how you can implement these techniques.

- Start by setting a timer for 25-minute work intervals using the Pomodoro Technique.

- Create a daily task list and block out time for each task in your calendar.

- Prioritize tasks based on urgency and importance, first tackling the most critical ones.

- For perfectionists, embracing imperfection and learning from mistakes is crucial. Set "good enough" standards rather than aiming for perfection.

- Practice self-compassion and self-acceptance, reminding yourself that it's okay to make mistakes and that progress is more important than perfection.

Consider the story of Andrea, an accountant who struggled with meeting deadlines due to her perfectionism. She used time blocking to structure her day, setting aside specific times for each task. This approach helped her stay focused and complete tasks more efficiently.

Another success story is Brad, a project manager who battled procrastination. He implemented the Pomodoro Technique, setting a timer for 25 minutes and working without distractions. Over time, he found that breaking tasks into smaller intervals made them more manageable, and his productivity soared.

Procrastination and perfectionism are formidable foes, but with the right strategies, you can overcome them. By breaking tasks into smaller steps, setting realistic goals, and embracing imperfection, you can combat procrastination and achieve greater success in your professional life.

Build Confidence in Professional Settings

Imagine entering a room filled with your colleagues, and you're scheduled to present a new project. Your palms sweat, your voice trembles, and your mind races with doubts. Professional confidence feels like a distant dream.

Confidence is crucial for career success and overcoming self-sabotage. It's not just about feeling good; it's about performing well. Confidence equips you with the ability to take on leadership roles, make decisions swiftly, and inspire trust in others. It's the secret that makes you stand out in a crowded room.

Professional confidence has several key characteristics.

- It's about believing in your abilities, even when faced with challenges.

- It manifests in your actions, from how you carry yourself to how you communicate.

- Confident professionals are more likely to take on leadership roles because they trust their judgment and skills.

- This trust translates into better decision-making, as they're not paralyzed by fear or doubt. They can weigh options quickly and act decisively, which is valuable in any professional setting.

On the flip side, low confidence can be a career killer.

- When you lack confidence, you hesitate to take on new challenges, fearing failure.

- This hesitation can make you miss out on opportunities for growth and advancement.

- You might find it difficult to assert yourself or negotiate for what you deserve, whether a raise, a promotion, or even credit for your work.

- This reluctance can lead to frustration and stagnation as you watch others advance while you remain stuck in the same spot.

Building and Maintaining Professional Confidence

Building and maintaining professional confidence requires deliberate effort.

1. **Set and achieve small, incremental goals**. Start with tasks just outside your comfort zone and gradually take on more challenging ones. Each success builds your confidence, creating a positive feedback loop.

2. **Seek mentorship and professional development opportunities**, which make a huge difference. A mentor can provide valuable insights, encouragement, and constructive criticism, helping you grow personally and professionally.

3. **Practice assertiveness and effective communication**. Assertiveness isn't about being aggressive; it's about expressing your thoughts and needs clearly and respectfully. Effective communication ensures that your ideas are heard and valued.

4. **Visualization** is a powerful tool for building confidence. Before a big meeting or presentation, take a few moments to visualize yourself succeeding. Picture every detail, including the room, the audience, and your confident delivery. This mental rehearsal can boost your confidence and reduce anxiety.

5. **Positive affirmations** can also be incredibly effective. Create affirmations specific to your professional achievements, such as "I am a capable leader" or "I excel in my role." Repeat these affirmations daily to reinforce your self-belief.

6. **Seek feedback and constructive criticism** from colleagues to help you identify areas for improvement and build on your strengths. It's important to view feedback as a tool for growth rather than a personal attack.

Exercises

Let's get practical with some exercises to build your confidence.

7E. Start with role-playing scenarios for public speaking.

- Practice your presentation in front of a friend or family member and ask for feedback.

- This exercise can help you become more comfortable and confident in front of an audience.

7F. Writing and repeating professional affirmations is another simple but effective exercise.

- Set aside a few minutes each day to write down your affirmations and say them out loud.

7G. Setting up a feedback loop with colleagues can also be beneficial.

- Share your goals with a trusted colleague and ask them to provide regular feedback on your progress.

- This accountability can help you stay on track and continuously improve.

Consider the story of Rhonda, a consulting manager who struggled with confidence in public speaking. She began practicing her presentations in front of trusted colleagues, gradually building her confidence. Over time, she became a more effective and confident speaker, positively impacting her career.

Another example is Maurice, a government leader who improved his confidence by taking on challenging projects. He sought mentorship and continually pushed himself out of his comfort zone. This proactive approach helped him grow as a leader and gain the respect of his team.

Lastly, there's Arad, an engineer who used positive affirmations to boost his confidence. He wrote affirmations like "I am an expert in my field" and repeated them daily. This practice helped him overcome self-doubt and achieve greater career success.

Use Effective Time Management

Imagine you're at your desk, staring at a mountain of tasks and feeling like you're drowning in a sea of responsibilities. Your mind is racing, and you can't seem to get started despite the urgency.

Time management for overthinkers is like oxygen for a diver; it can mean the difference between thriving and floundering. Effective time management reduces stress, prevents feelings of overwhelm, and enhances productivity and focus. It's not just about getting things done; it's about creating a structured environment where you can perform at your best without feeling like you're constantly running behind.

The **Eisenhower Matrix,** discussed in Chapter 3, is one of the most effective tools for managing your time.

By categorizing your tasks based on urgency and importance, you can focus on what matters and delegate or eliminate the rest. For example, responding to a critical client email might fall under urgent and important, while planning a long-term project could be important but not urgent. This approach helps you allocate your time wisely and avoid the trap of overthinking minor tasks.

The **Two-Minute Rule** is another handy technique. If a task can be done in two minutes or less, do it immediately. This rule is brilliant for handling quick tasks that clutter your to-do list and drain your mental energy. Whether responding to a short email or filing a document, tackling these small tasks right away can free up mental space and keep you moving forward. It's a simple yet powerful way to prevent procrastination and maintain momentum.

Use a planner or digital calendar for effective time management. Templates for a planner like the one illustrated here are available in Microsoft Excel.

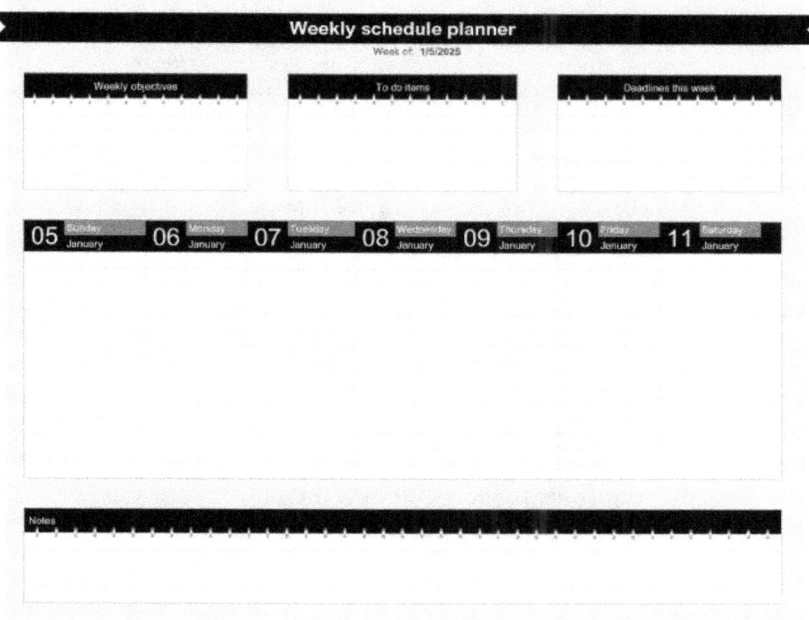

Whether you prefer a physical or digital planner, having a visual representation of your schedule can help you stay organized and focused. A planner allows you to block out time for specific tasks, set deadlines, and track your progress. Digital calendars have the added benefit of setting reminders and alerts, ensuring you never miss a deadline or forget an important meeting. Planning your day can reduce the anxiety of last-minute rushes and create a more structured, manageable workflow.

Exercises

Here's how you can put these strategies into practice.

7H. Start by creating a daily to-do list using the Eisenhower Matrix.

- List and categorize all your tasks based on their urgency and importance.
- This will give you a clear picture of your priorities and help you focus on what needs immediate attention.

7I. Next, apply the Two-Minute Rule to handle small tasks right away.

- This will keep your to-do list manageable and allow you to maintain a steady pace.

7J. Finally, set reminders and alerts for important tasks and deadlines in your digital calendar.

- This will ensure you stay on track and manage your time effectively.

Consider the story of Jennifer, a hair salon owner struggling to prioritize her tasks. She started using the Eisenhower Matrix to categorize her daily responsibilities. Focusing first on urgent and important tasks significantly reduced her stress levels and improved her productivity.

Another success story is Jake, a teacher drowning in administrative work. He began using a digital planner to block out time for different tasks and set reminders for deadlines and important meetings. This approach helped him stay organized and manage his time more efficiently, allowing him to focus on his students and teaching.

Effective time management is a game-changer for overthinkers. By immediately prioritizing tasks, handling quick tasks, and using planners or digital calendars, you can reduce stress, enhance productivity, and regain control over your professional life.

Real-Life Examples of Professional Success

Learning from case studies is like peeking into someone else's playbook. It's incredibly valuable to see how others have navigated their professional challenges, especially when they face obstacles similar to yours. By studying real-life examples of career success, you can gain practical insights and find inspiration to tackle your hurdles. These stories provide a roadmap, showing you what works, what doesn't, and how persistence can turn things around.

Case Study A - Perfectionism

We'll start with the story of Erin, a human resources administrator who struggled with perfectionism. She was so focused on making everything flawless that she often worked late and felt burnt out. Erin realized that her perfectionism was holding her back from leadership roles. She decided to set clear goals and focus on progress rather than perfection. By prioritizing tasks and seeking feedback, Erin was able to advance in her career, eventually becoming an HR manager. Her journey highlights the importance of setting realistic expectations and leveraging strengths.

Case Study B – Entrepreneur's Self-Sabotage

Mitchell is a technology startup founder who built a successful company from scratch. Mitchell faced numerous setbacks, from funding issues to market competition. He resolved to identify self-sabotage behaviors and overcome them. Mitchell practiced confidence-building techniques and set clear, achievable goals. He also sought mentorship and built a support network. This approach not only helped him stay focused but also allowed him to leverage his strengths and seek support when needed. Mitchell's story is a testament to the power of resilience and continuous learning.

Case Study C – Academic Researcher with Imposter Syndrome

Academia has its challenges, as Tricia, a researcher, can attest. Despite her impressive credentials, Tricia struggled with imposter syndrome, constantly doubting her abilities. She decided to tackle this head-on by setting incremental goals and seeking feedback from her peers. Tricia also practiced effective time management, using tools like the Eisenhower Matrix to prioritize her tasks. Her efforts paid off, and she eventually achieved recognition in her field. Tricia's experience underscores the importance of seeking feedback for self-awareness to overcome professional obstacles.

Case Study D – Artist's Self-Sabotage

In the creative industries, we have Arthur, an artist who turned his passion into a thriving career. Arthur faced numerous obstacles, from self-doubt to financial instability. He identified his self-sabotage behaviors and worked on building his confidence. Arthur set clear goals and leveraged his strengths, seeking support from fellow artists and mentors. He practiced effective time management, ensuring he dedicated enough time to both his creative work and business aspects. Arthur's story is a reminder that persistence and a strategic approach can turn passion into a successful career.

Case Study E – Salesperson with Procrastination

Sabrina is a salesperson who struggled with procrastination. She knew she had the skills to excel but found herself constantly putting off tasks. She decided to implement the Pomodoro Technique and time blocking to stay focused. She also set clear goals and sought accountability partners to keep her on track. Over time, her sales numbers improved, and she gained recognition in her company. Sabrina's experience highlights the importance of setting realistic goals and using effective time management techniques to overcome procrastination.

Common Strategies

Analyzing these case studies reveals several common strategies.

- Identifying self-sabotage behaviors is the first step toward overcoming them.

- Setting clear goals and seeking feedback builds confidence, which is a crucial role.

- Leveraging strengths and seeking support from mentors and peers can provide valuable guidance and encouragement.

- Effective time management ensures that tasks are prioritized and completed efficiently.

Lessons Learned

The lessons learned from these stories are clear.

- Self-awareness, resilience, and perseverance are key to overcoming professional challenges.

- Taking calculated risks and seizing opportunities can lead to significant growth.

- Persistence in applying new techniques, continuous learning, and adaptation are essential for long-term success.

- Seeking feedback and support can provide valuable insights and help you stay on track.

Action Items

So, what can you take away from these stories?

- Set realistic goals and milestones to keep yourself motivated and focused.

- Build a support network of mentors and peers who can provide guidance and encouragement.

- Continually assess your strategies and adjust as needed.

- Remember, it's about progress, not perfection, and every small step you take brings you closer to your professional goals.

In the next chapter, we will explore how to strengthen your personal relationships by understanding and managing overthinking in social interactions. This will help you build more meaningful connections and improve your overall well-being.

CHAPTER 8

STRENGTHEN PERSONAL RELATIONSHIPS

Imagine you're at a dinner party, and someone starts talking about a new project at work. Your mind immediately starts racing. "Did I say the right thing in that meeting today? What if they think I'm incompetent? Should I have sent that email differently?" Before you know it, you're nodding to the conversation but not hearing a word. Overthinking has hijacked your social skills, and now you're stuck in your head instead of enjoying the moment.

This chapter will explore how you can strengthen relationships by managing overthinking and improving communication.

Communication Strategies for Overthinkers

Effective communication is the bedrock of any strong relationship. When you're prone to overthinking, clear communication becomes even more crucial.

- Overthinking can lead to miscommunication because you're constantly second-guessing yourself.

- You might interpret a neutral comment as a criticism or hesitate to express your feelings, fearing you'll say the wrong thing.

- This can create a web of misunderstandings that strain your relationships.

Improving your communication skills can reduce these misunderstandings and build stronger, more meaningful connections.

- **Active listening** is one of the most effective ways to improve communication. This means focusing entirely on the person speaking rather than formulating your response while they're talking.

- **Maintain eye contact** to show you're engaged and interested.

- **Use "I" statements** to express your feelings, such as "I felt hurt when..." instead of "You made me feel...", which can come off as accusatory. This shifts the focus from blaming to sharing your perspective, fostering a more open and constructive dialogue.

- **Avoid accusations and blame** by being specific and direct about what's bothering you. Instead of saying, "You never listen to me," try, "I feel unheard when I share my thoughts, and there's no response."

- **Reflective listening** is another powerful tool. This involves repeating what the other person said to show you understand. For example, if your friend says, "I'm really stressed about work," you might respond,

"It sounds like work has been very overwhelming for you." This not only shows you're listening but also helps clarify any misunderstandings.

- **Ask open-ended questions** to encourage deeper conversations. Instead of asking, "Did you have a good day?" try, "What was the best part of your day?"

- **Paraphrasing and summarizing** what you've heard can also ensure clarity. For example, "So, you're saying that the meeting didn't go as planned, and you're worried about the outcome?" This technique can prevent miscommunication and ensure you're both on the same page.

- **Non-verbal communication** is just as important. Your body language, facial expressions, and tone of voice convey messages. Be mindful of these cues to ensure they align with your words.

Exercises

8A. To practice these skills, try role-playing difficult conversations. This can help you rehearse and become more comfortable expressing your thoughts and feelings.

8B. The "I" statement exercise is another useful tool. Write down common complaints you have and rephrase them using "I" statements.

8C. Daily check-ins with your partner or close friends can strengthen communication. Take a few minutes daily to share what's on your mind, listen actively, and reflect on what you've heard.

Consider the story of Amy and Spencer, a couple who struggled with constant misunderstandings. They decided to practice active listening by setting aside time each evening to discuss their day. Amy used "I" statements to express her feelings, and Spencer practiced reflective listening. Over time, they found that their conflicts decreased, and their bond grew stronger.

Similarly, Debbie and Christina, best friends since college, noticed their friendship becoming strained due to busy schedules and miscommunication. They started doing weekly check-ins, sharing updates, asking open-ended questions, and reflecting on each other's thoughts. This simple practice helped them reconnect and strengthen their friendship.

Improving your communication skills can transform your relationships. You can reduce misunderstandings and build deeper connections by being an active listener, expressing your feelings clearly, and practicing reflective listening. So, remember these strategies next time you find yourself spiraling into overthinking. They can help you stay present, communicate effectively, and strengthen your personal relationships.

Set Healthy Boundaries

Definition: Healthy boundaries are like invisible lines that define what's acceptable and what's not in any relationship.

Think of personal boundaries as your space bubble, not just physical but emotional and mental. They help you protect your well-being and maintain your identity.

Boundaries come in many forms: emotional, physical, time, and digital.

Emotional boundaries involve not taking on others' emotions as your own.

Physical boundaries can be as simple as needing personal space or privacy. Setting these boundaries is essential because they foster mutual respect and understanding. But when you're an overthinker, setting boundaries can feel like walking a tightrope. You worry about how others will react, fearing rejection or conflict.

Time boundaries involve protecting your time and ensuring others respect it. For example, limit how much time you're willing to spend on work tasks after hours or how much time you allocate to social activities. Suppose someone consistently asks you for your time, violating your boundaries. In that case, you can kindly but firmly decline by saying, "I'm not available at that time, but I can help you tomorrow," or "I need to finish my other obligations before we talk."

Digital boundaries refer to how you manage your online interactions and screen time. This includes limiting your digital use, including how often you check emails or social media to avoid becoming overwhelmed. Digital boundaries also include respecting others' digital privacy. For example, you should avoid oversharing someone's personal stories or information without their consent and refrain from tagging people in photos or posts if they've asked you not to. Setting these boundaries helps maintain trust and respect in your online relationships.

Exercises

8D. To identify your boundaries, start by reflecting on past experiences where you felt uncomfortable or resentful. These feelings are often indicators that your boundaries were crossed.

- Grab a journal and jot down instances when you felt these emotions.

- Ask yourself, "What happened? How did I feel? What boundary was crossed?"

- This exercise can help you pinpoint your limits.

8E. Identifying boundary violations is another crucial step.

- Notice when you feel drained or taken advantage of, as these are signs that your boundaries need reinforcing.

Setting boundaries can be challenging. Fear of rejection or causing conflict can make it daunting. You might feel guilty, thinking you're being selfish or unreasonable. But remember, setting boundaries is about self-respect, not shutting people out. It's about creating a space to thrive while maintaining healthy relationships.

- **Use assertive communication,** which is vital. Use clear and respectful language to express your needs. For example, say, "I need some quiet time after work to decompress," instead of, "You're always so loud when I get home."

- **Be consistent and firm**. The "broken record" technique of repeating your needs calmly and consistently can be very effective. If someone pushes back, stay polite but firm. "I understand you enjoy loud music in the evening, but I need quiet time to relax. Can we find a compromise?"

- Plan to **handle pushback and resistance**; it's part of the process. Not everyone will be happy with your boundaries, and that's okay. Stick to your plan and remember why you set those boundaries in the first place.

- **Set consequences** if someone repeatedly violates your boundaries despite your efforts. This might mean limiting your interactions with them or seeking mediation if the relationship is crucial but strained.

Maintaining healthy boundaries can transform your relationships and personal well-being. You'll notice increased respect and understanding from others because they know where you stand. You'll also experience reduced stress and overthinking because you're not constantly worried about others intruding. This newfound clarity can enhance your self-esteem and autonomy, giving you the confidence to assert your needs without guilt.

Take Michelle, a private equities executive who struggled with work-life balance. She found herself working late hours and answering emails at all times. Feeling overwhelmed, she decided to set boundaries by not checking emails after 7 p.m. and turning off work notifications. Her colleagues initially resisted, but she remained firm. Over time, they respected her boundaries, and Michelle found herself more relaxed and productive.

Or consider Vic, who had difficulty setting boundaries in his romantic relationship. He felt smothered by his partner's constant need for attention. Vic communicated his need for personal space, using "I" statements to express his feelings. His partner was initially hurt but eventually understood and respected his needs. This improved their relationship and allowed Vic to feel more at ease.

Setting and maintaining healthy boundaries is a powerful tool for improving your relationships and overall well-being. It takes practice and perseverance, but the rewards are worth the effort.

Conflict Resolution without Overthinking

Overthinking can turn a minor disagreement into a full-blown conflict. Imagine having a small disagreement with your partner about who forgot to take out the trash. What starts as a simple issue spirals into a mental maze of "Do they think I'm lazy?" and "What if this means our relationship is doomed?"

Overthinking complicates and prolongs conflicts by leading to misinterpretations and escalating emotions. Your mind races through worst-case scenarios, making it difficult to see the situation clearly. This mental fog impacts your emotional well-being, leaving you stressed and anxious. It can also strain your relationship dynamics, creating a cycle of misunderstanding and resentment.

Effective conflict resolution techniques are essential for navigating these turbulent waters.

- One of the most crucial steps is to **stay calm and composed**. When emotions run high, take a deep breath and allow yourself a moment to cool down. This pause can prevent knee-jerk reactions and give you time to gather your thoughts.

- **Active listening and empathy** are powerful tools in resolving conflicts. Instead of focusing on your perspective, try to understand the other person's point of view. This doesn't mean you must agree, but acknowledging their feelings can diffuse tension.

- **Collaborative problem-solving techniques** are also valuable. Approach the conflict as a team effort to find a solution that works for both parties. This shifts the focus from blame to resolution, fostering a sense of partnership.

Managing your thoughts during conflicts is key to preventing overthinking from derailing the resolution process.

- Mindfulness practices can help you stay present and focused on the current situation rather than spiral into negative thought patterns.

- Simple techniques like **deep breathing or grounding exercises** can anchor you in the moment, making it easier to handle the conflict calmly. Focus on something tangible, like the sensation of your feet on the ground or the sound of your breath. This can interrupt negative spirals and keep you grounded.

- **Thought-stopping techniques** are another effective strategy. When you notice your mind wandering into overthinking, mentally say "stop" and redirect to the present situation.

Consider the story of the Martinez family. They used to argue frequently, with conflicts often escalating to the point where no one remembered the original issue. The turning point came when they decided to address conflicts calmly. During a heated argument about household chores, they implemented a new rule: anyone feeling overwhelmed could call a "time-out," allowing everyone to cool down before continuing the discussion.

They also practiced active listening, with each family member taking turns speaking without interruption. This simple change made a world of difference. They found that when everyone felt heard and understood, they were more willing to compromise and find solutions. Conflicts that once dragged on for days were resolved in hours, and the overall atmosphere at home became more peaceful and cooperative.

Manage Relationship Doubts

Relationship doubts often spring from a deep well of fear and uncertainty.

- Fear of vulnerability is a major culprit. You might worry that opening up will expose you, making it easier for someone to hurt you.

- Past relationship trauma can also rear its ugly head, causing you to doubt even the most solid connections. Maybe you were betrayed or abandoned before, and now you're constantly looking for signs that history will repeat itself.

- Low self-esteem can further fuel these doubts. You're more likely to second-guess your partner's intentions and actions when you don't feel worthy of love or respect.

- Overthinking exacerbates these doubts, turning minor concerns into monumental issues. A casual comment can spiral into a full-blown crisis in your mind, making it hard to see things clearly.

Reducing relationship doubts requires a multi-pronged approach.

- **Cognitive restructuring** is a powerful technique for challenging negative thoughts. When you catch yourself thinking, "They're going to leave me," ask yourself, "What evidence do I have for this?" Breaking down these thoughts can help you see them for what they are—unfounded fears.

- **Building self-awareness through mindfulness** is another effective strategy. By staying present, you can observe your thoughts without getting swept away. This can help you identify patterns and triggers, making it easier to manage your doubts.

- **Open and honest communication** with your partner is also crucial. Share your feelings and concerns without accusing or blaming. This not only clears the air but also strengthens your emotional bond.

Exercises

Working through exercises for self-reflection can further help you address relationship doubts.

8F. Reflective journaling prompts can provide valuable insights. Find a quiet place to reflect and write about these questions.

- What are my biggest fears in this relationship?

- When did I last feel secure, and why?

8G. Writing letters to yourself can help you process your feelings and gain a more balanced perspective.

- Write a letter to yourself about your doubts.

- Write another letter to yourself in response, addressing the doubts with compassion and logic.

Consider the story of Yana, who struggled with severe trust issues after a previous relationship ended in betrayal. She constantly doubted her new partner, questioning his every move. Yana decided to tackle her doubts head-on. She began by practicing cognitive restructuring, challenging her negative thoughts with evidence of her partner's trustworthiness. She also incorporated mindfulness practices, spending a few minutes each day observing her thoughts without judgment. Open communication also played a crucial role. Yana shared her fears with her partner, who responded with understanding and reassurance. Over time, her trust issues diminished, and she felt more secure in the relationship.

Another example is Pedro and Vanessa, who both doubted their future together. They decided to work through their doubts by setting aside time each week for open and honest conversations. Each one used reflective journaling to explore their fears and concerns, then they shared their insights with each other. Writing letters to themselves helped them process their emotions and gain clarity. This mutual effort alleviated their doubts and brought them closer together.

Managing relationship doubts is a continuous process. You can reduce doubts and strengthen your relationship by challenging negative thoughts, building self-awareness, and communicating openly. Exercises like reflective journaling and writing letters to yourself can provide additional support, helping you gain clarity and peace of mind.

Build Trust and Confidence in Relationships

Trust and confidence are the cornerstones of any healthy relationship. Without them, emotional safety crumbles, cooperation dwindles, and overall relationship satisfaction takes a nosedive. Imagine trying to build a house without a solid foundation; it won't stand the test of time. The same goes for relationships.

Trust creates a safe space where both partners feel secure and valued, making it easier to open up and share. It also enhances cooperation. When you trust each other, you're more likely to work together, tackling challenges head-on instead of butting heads. Finally, confidence in your relationship can significantly boost satisfaction. Knowing that you can rely on your partner and that they can rely on you brings a sense of stability and happiness.

Action Items

Building this trust and confidence takes effort but is well worth it.

- One effective way to build trust is by sharing personal thoughts and feelings. This doesn't mean you have to spill your deepest secrets immediately, but opening up about your day-to-day experiences, dreams, and fears can create a stronger emotional bond.

- Engaging in meaningful conversations where you both feel heard and understood can deepen your connection.

- Make time for physical affection and quality time together. The physical touch of a hug, a kiss, or holding hands can reinforce feelings of love and security.

- Plan date nights or weekend getaways to focus solely on each other, away from daily distractions.

- Shared goal-setting is a fantastic way to build trust and confidence. Sit down with your partner and discuss your individual goals and your goals as a couple. These could be anything from planning a vacation to buying a house or even starting a family.

- Regular relationship check-ins can help you stay aligned and address any issues before they become major problems. Take time each week or month to discuss how you feel about the relationship, what's going well, and what could be improved. This consistent communication keeps you both on the same page and shows you're committed to making the relationship work.

Increasing relationship confidence involves being honest and transparent with each other. If something's bothering you, don't bottle it up. Practicing vulnerability can be scary but incredibly rewarding. It allows you to connect on a deeper level and fosters trust. Keeping promises and commitments is crucial. If you say you're going to do something, follow through. This builds reliability and shows that you can count on each other. Showing consistency in your actions, whether being there when you say you will be or supporting your partner's endeavors, reinforces trust.

Exercises

Trust-building exercises can be helpful.

8H. Try activities that require teamwork and communication, like cooking a meal together or tackling a home project.

8I. Plan and engage in shared activities you enjoy, whether hiking, attending a concert, or watching a movie.

8J. Celebrate relationship milestones, like anniversaries or personal achievements. Reflect on how far you've come and the challenges you've overcome together.

8K. Use positive affirmations for relationship success. Remind yourself and your partner of your relationship's strengths and positive aspects. Simple phrases like, "We make a great team" or "I appreciate everything you do" can reinforce your bond.

Consider the story of Denine and Jack, who faced a significant breach of trust when Jack admitted to chatting frequently over social media with a former high school girlfriend. They decided to rebuild their trust by being completely transparent about their friends and setting boundaries. Regular check-ins and open conversations helped them regain confidence in each other.

Think about Lucia and Abe, friends who drifted apart due to busy lives. They decided to reconnect by engaging in shared activities like weekend hikes and regular coffee dates. These experiences brought them closer, and they even started a small business together, strengthening their bond through mutual goals and trust.

Real-Life Stories of Relationship Success

Couple Arguing

Let's start with the story of Carlos and Maria, a couple who used to find themselves locked in heated arguments over the most minor issues. They realized that their communication was the root of the problem.

They decided to take a proactive approach by enrolling in a communication workshop. There, they learned techniques like active listening and using "I" statements. By focusing on expressing their feelings rather than assigning blame, their conflicts became less frequent and more manageable. Over time, their relationship grew stronger, and they began to understand each other more deeply.

The key takeaway is the value of learning and practicing effective communication methods. Their consistent effort paid off, reducing misunderstandings and building a more harmonious relationship.

Lack of Time for a Friend

Next, let's talk about Ben and Samuel, best friends since college who found their relationship strained as they entered their 30s. They juggled demanding jobs and personal commitments, leaving little time to get together.

They decided to set healthy boundaries for other demands of their time and prioritize their friendship. They scheduled regular weekly catchups, alternating between virtual and in-person meet-ups. They also established clear boundaries about discussing work-related stress so they could dedicate their time together to more uplifting conversations. This conscious effort to set and maintain boundaries deepened their bond and made their time together more enjoyable.

The lesson is the value of prioritizing relationships and setting boundaries to protect them.

Couple with Trust Issues

Now, consider the story of Jack and Drew, who struggled with trust issues after Drew admitted to hiding financial difficulties. They decided to rebuild their relationship by being completely transparent about their finances and setting shared financial goals.

They began with small steps, like creating a budget together and scheduling regular financial check-ins. These trust-building activities helped them regain confidence in each other and strengthened their emotional bond. They also found that celebrating small victories, like paying off a credit card, reinforced their commitment to each other.

The main takeaway is that trust can be rebuilt through consistent, transparent actions and shared goals.

Friends with Unspoken Resentments

Finally, let's look at the story of Liz and Rebecca, friends who drifted apart due to misunderstandings and unspoken resentments. They addressed their issues head-on by having an open and honest conversation.

They used active listening techniques to ensure they both felt heard and understood. They also made a pact to check in regularly and be transparent about their feelings. This new approach transformed their friendship, making it stronger and more resilient.

The lesson is the importance of open communication and regular check-ins to maintain and strengthen relationships.

Each of these stories highlights different strategies for building and maintaining strong relationships. Whether it's improving communication, setting boundaries, rebuilding trust, or fostering open dialogue, the common theme is consistent effort and mutual respect. Applying these insights to your relationships can create deeper, more meaningful connections. Regular check-ins, celebrating small victories, and practicing active listening are practical steps to strengthen your relationships.

Next, we'll explore how to take a more holistic approach to eliminating overthinking and self-sabotage.

CHAPTER 9

HOLISTIC APPROACHES TO MANAGE OVERTHINKING

I magine standing in front of the refrigerator, staring blankly at its contents, wondering if that leftover pizza is a good idea for dinner. Your brain is already foggy from a long day, and cooking something homemade feels like climbing Mount Everest. Did you know that what you eat can help clear that mental fog? Yes, your diet significantly affects how you think and feel. Let's dive into how you can use food to manage overthinking and boost mental clarity.

Understand the Role of Diet in Mental Health

You might not realize it, but your brain is a high-maintenance organ. It needs a constant supply of fuel, and the quality of that fuel directly affects its performance. Think of your brain as a luxury car; you wouldn't put low-grade fuel in a Ferrari, would you? Similarly, your brain runs best on high-quality foods that contain essential vitamins, minerals, and antioxidants. These nutrients nourish and protect your brain from oxidative stress, which is like rust for your brain cells.

Macronutrients and micronutrients play a crucial role in this.

- Macronutrients, including proteins, fats, and carbohydrates, provide the energy your brain needs to function.
  - Proteins are broken down into amino acids, which are the building blocks of neurotransmitters, those chemical messengers that keep your brain ticking.
  - Healthy fats, like omega-3 fatty acids, are vital for maintaining cell membrane flexibility and supporting cognitive functions.
  - Carbohydrates, particularly complex carbs, offer a steady supply of glucose, the primary energy source for your brain.
- Micronutrients, although needed in smaller amounts, are no less important.
  - Vitamins and minerals, such as the various B vitamins, vitamin D, magnesium, and zinc, are essential for numerous brain functions, from energy production to neurotransmitter synthesis.
  - A balanced diet incorporating these nutrients ensures your brain has everything it needs to operate at its best.

Some foods are especially beneficial for mental health and can help reduce overthinking.

- Omega-3 fatty acids in fatty fish such as salmon, trout, and sardines are excellent for brain health. They support learning, memory, and overall cognitive function.

- Antioxidant-rich foods like blueberries, nuts, and dark chocolate protect your brain from oxidative damage and improve memory.

- Complex carbohydrates, such as whole grains and legumes, provide a slow and steady release of glucose, helping maintain mental clarity and focus.

On the flip side, certain foods and dietary habits can exacerbate overthinking and anxiety.

- High sugar intake, for example, can lead to energy spikes and crashes, affecting mood and cognitive function.

- Excessive caffeine consumption can increase anxiety and disrupt sleep, which in turn fuels overthinking.

- Processed foods and trans fats are also bad for you. They can cause inflammation and negatively impact brain health, leading to impaired cognitive function and increased anxiety.

So, how do you incorporate more brain-healthy foods into your daily meals? Start with meal planning. Dedicate some time each week to plan balanced meals that include a variety of macronutrients and micronutrients.

- For breakfast, consider a bowl of oatmeal topped with berries and a sprinkle of flaxseeds. This combo offers complex carbs, antioxidants, and omega-3s.

- For lunch, a salmon salad with mixed greens, avocado, and a handful of walnuts provides healthy fats, vitamins, and minerals.

- Dinner could be a hearty quinoa and vegetable stir-fry, delivering a mix of complex carbs, fiber, and essential nutrients.

- Snacks can also be an opportunity to boost your mental clarity. Instead of reaching for chips or candy, opt for brain-boosting options like a handful of almonds, a piece of dark chocolate (aim for 70% cocoa or higher), or some sliced apple with peanut butter. These snacks balance healthy fats, antioxidants, and protein, keeping your brain fueled and focused.

- For a quick and nutritious pick-me-up, try blending up a brain-boosting smoothie. Combine a handful of spinach, a cup of blueberries, half an avocado, a tablespoon of flaxseeds, and some almond milk. This smoothie is packed with antioxidants, healthy fats, and vitamins, offering a delicious way to support your mental health.

To make things easier, here's a quick checklist:

BRAIN-BOOSTING FOODS CHECKLIST

- **Omega-3 fatty acids:** Salmon, trout, sardines, flaxseeds
- **Antioxidant-rich foods:** Blueberries, nuts, dark chocolate
- **Complex carbohydrates:** Whole grains, legumes
- **Micronutrient-rich foods:** Spinach, broccoli, pumpkin seeds, eggs

Incorporating these foods into your diet can help improve your brain function, reduce overthinking, and support overall mental health. Remember, your brain is like a luxury car—give it the premium fuel it deserves, and you'll notice the difference.

EXERCISES

9A. Take the time to plan healthy meals and snacks for the coming week that include a balanced variety of macronutrients and micronutrients.

Get Physical Exercise for Mental Clarity

Imagine you're at the end of a long, grueling day. Your mind feels like a tangled mess of to-do lists and worries. Moving your body might seem like an extra chore, but trust me, it's a game-changer for mental clarity.

Exercise can be a powerful antidote to overthinking. When you get moving, your brain releases endorphins—those feel-good chemicals that act like natural mood lifters. Think of endorphins as tiny cheerleaders in your brain, boosting your mood and making you feel more relaxed. Exercise lowers cortisol levels, the stress hormone that fuels anxiety and overthinking.

Regular physical activity doesn't just perk up your mood; it also helps improve sleep quality. A good workout tires out your body, making it easier to fall asleep and stay asleep. We all know how much better everything seems after a solid night's rest. When you exercise, your brain gets a boost of oxygen and nutrients, improving cognitive functions like memory and focus. It's like powering your brain, helping you think more clearly and make better decisions.

So, what types of exercise are best for mental clarity?

- **Aerobic exercises**, such as running, cycling, or even brisk walking, are fantastic for raising your heart rate and flooding your brain with oxygen.

- **Strength training**, such as weightlifting, builds muscle and releases endorphins that lift your mood.

- **Mind-body exercises** like yoga and tai chi are particularly beneficial. They combine physical movement with mindfulness, helping you stay present and focused while reducing stress and anxiety.

The science behind exercise and mental health is fascinating. When you exercise, your heart pumps more blood to your brain, delivering much-needed oxygen and nutrients. This increased blood flow stimulates the production of new neural connections, a process known as neurogenesis. Think of it as growing new pathways in your brain, making it more flexible and resilient. Exercise also enhances neurotransmitter function, increasing serotonin, dopamine, and norepinephrine levels—chemicals that regulate mood and anxiety.

Incorporating exercise into your daily routine doesn't have to be complicated.

EXERCISES

9B. Start by creating a **weekly workout plan**.

- Schedule specific times for your workouts, just like you would for any other important appointment.

- Find activities you enjoy to stay motivated. If you hate running, don't force it; try dancing, swimming, or even hiking.

- Combine different types of exercise to keep things interesting and provide holistic benefits. For example, you might do yoga on Mondays, strength training on Wednesdays, and a long walk or run on Saturdays.

- Tracking your progress using apps and tools can also be motivating. Apps like Strava, MyFitnessPal, or even a simple journal can help you set goals and celebrate your achievements.

Let's look at some real-life examples. Take Margaret, who struggled with anxiety for years. She found that regular yoga practice helped her manage her anxiety. Combining physical movement and mindfulness allowed her to stay grounded and present, reducing her overthinking.

Then there's Vijay, a busy accountant with a jam-packed schedule. He started integrating short workouts into his daily routine, like a 15-minute HIIT session (high-intensity interval training) in the morning and a quick walk during lunch breaks. These small bursts of activity greatly impacted his mental clarity and overall stress levels.

Exercise doesn't have to be a daunting task. It's about finding what works for you and making it a consistent part of your life. Whether it's a morning run, a dance class, or a relaxing yoga session, moving your body can help clear your mind and reduce overthinking. So, lace up those sneakers or roll out that yoga mat—your brain will thank you.

Develop a Balanced Lifestyle

Imagine juggling work emails, trying to recall whether you fed the dog, and wondering when you'll have time to call your mom. Your brain feels like a web browser with too many tabs open. Suppose you could close some of those tabs and find some peace. A balanced lifestyle can help you do just that. It's not about perfection but finding harmony among all the different parts of your life.

Components of a balanced lifestyle include work-life balance, social connections, and time for hobbies and relaxation.

- **Work-life balance** means setting boundaries between your job and personal life. It's crucial to avoid burnout and ensure you're not just living to work.

- **Social connections** are equally important. Humans are social creatures, and maintaining meaningful relationships can boost your mental health and reduce overthinking.

- **Making time for hobbies and relaxation** is essential. Whether reading, gardening, or binge-watching your favorite show, these activities provide a much-needed mental break.

Recognizing areas of imbalance in your life is the first step toward achieving balance.

Exercises

9C. Reflective journaling can be a powerful tool for this.

- Spend a few minutes each day writing about your activities and how they made you feel.

- Do you spend too much time on work and not enough on yourself?

9D. Self-assessment online quizzes and questionnaires can help you identify which areas of your life need more attention.

- Open an internet browser and search for "quiz to determine if my lifestyle is balanced." You'll find many options from health and well-being organizations.

- Select and complete a few quizzes to identify where your life lacks balance.

Once you've identified the imbalances, it's time to take action.

9E. Start by setting boundaries between work and personal life.

- This might mean not checking work emails after a certain time or dedicating weekends to family and personal activities.

9F. Prioritize self-care activities.

- Plan time for things like exercise, meditation, or even just taking a long bath.

- These activities may seem small but can significantly impact your mental health.

9G. Scheduling regular social activities is also crucial.

- Make time for the people who matter to you, whether it's a weekly coffee date with a friend or a monthly family dinner.

Let's look at some real-life success stories. Take Ruth, a corporate lawyer who was persistently stressed and needed more time for herself. She started by setting clear boundaries at work, such as not answering emails after 7 PM. She also scheduled regular yoga classes and made it a point to have dinner with her family every night. Over time, Ruth found that she was less stressed and more productive at work.

Consider Bill, a busy father who wanted to spend more time on his hobbies. He carved out a couple of hours every weekend to work on his car, something he loved but never had time for. This small change made him happier and more relaxed, positively affecting his family life.

By taking these steps, you can achieve a more balanced lifestyle, reducing stress and overthinking. Whether setting boundaries, prioritizing self-care, or making time for social connections, these changes can significantly improve your overall well-being.

Recognize the Connection Between Physical and Mental Well-Being

You've probably heard the phrase, "Healthy body, healthy mind," but what does that mean? Let's break it down.

- Your physical health and mental well-being are deeply interconnected like dance partners; when one stumbles, the other will likely trip.

- Physical activity directly impacts mental clarity. When you move your body, your brain gets a fresh supply of oxygen and nutrients, which can help clear the fog and sharpen your focus.

- Sleep also plays a significant role in this dance. Poor sleep can turn your brain into a sluggish mess, making it harder to manage stress and think clearly.

Recognizing when your physical health affects your mental well-being can be a game-changer. Chronic stress often manifests *physically* before you even realize what's happening *mentally*.

- Do you get frequent headaches or feel constant muscle tension? These could be signs that your stress levels are excessively high.

- Do you feel irritable and sluggish? This can be another red flag for a poor diet. Foods high in sugar and unhealthy fats can affect your mood and cognitive function.

- If you find yourself more mentally anxious or down than usual, look at what you're eating and how you're feeling physically.

- Regular health check-ups can catch issues like high blood pressure or nutritional deficiencies before they become more serious.

Holistic health practices can offer a two-for-one deal, benefiting your body and mind.

- Breathwork and meditation are great examples. These practices help lower stress levels, improve focus, and boost emotional well-being. Imagine starting your day with a few minutes of deep breathing; it's like hitting the reset button for your brain.

- Acupuncture and massage therapy are other fantastic options. They can help release built-up tension and improve circulation, leaving you feeling relaxed and rejuvenated.

- Walking meditation is a mindful movement practice that combines physical activity with mindfulness, helping you stay present while you move.

Exercises

Integrating holistic health practices into your daily life doesn't have to be complicated.

9H. Start by creating a morning routine with a few minutes of mindfulness and movement.

- This could be anything from stretching to a short meditation session.

9I. Plan time for regular health check-ups.

- These appointments can catch any physical issues that might be affecting your mental health.

9J. If you're comfortable with technology, consider adopting one of the holistic health apps and resources to help you stay on track.

- Apps like Calm or Headspace offer guided meditations.

- Apps like MyFitnessPal help you monitor your physical activity and diet.

These practices can make a big difference in how you feel daily. Imagine waking up, spending a few minutes on deep breathing, and then taking a mindful walk around your neighborhood. This simple routine can set a positive tone for your day, helping you manage stress and stay focused.

Recognizing the connection between physical health and mental well-being is essential for managing overthinking and reducing stress. Integrating holistic practices into your routine can improve physical and mental health, leading to a more balanced and fulfilling life.

Create Long-Term Healthy Habits

Imagine waking up every morning and automatically reaching for a glass of water, followed by a few minutes of stretching. You don't even think about it; it's just part of your routine. That's the power of habits. Developing long-term healthy habits is crucial for managing overthinking, and consistency is vital.

Habits reduce mental clutter by turning beneficial actions into automatic behaviors. You don't waste mental energy deciding whether to exercise or meditate; you just do it. This frees up mental space, making it easier to handle life's challenges without spiraling into overthinking.

The Habit Loop

Creating and maintaining healthy habits often involves understanding the habit loop: cue, routine, and reward. Let's break it down.

- The cue is what triggers the behavior. It could be something like waking up or feeling stressed.

- The routine is the behavior itself, such as meditating or going for a run.

- The reward is the benefit you get from the behavior, like feeling calm or energized.

By identifying these components, you can better understand and shape your habits.

Setting SMART goals (Specific, Measurable, Achievable, Relevant, and Time-bound) can also help. For example, instead of saying, "I want to exercise more," you might say, "I will go for a 20-minute walk every morning before work." This goal is clear, realistic, and easy to track.

Habit-tracking tools can be incredibly helpful. Apps like **Habitica** or simple habit trackers in your journal can keep you accountable. Seeing your progress visually can be motivating. It's like giving yourself a gold star for every day you stick to your new habit.

Remember: habits don't form overnight.

- **Start with small, manageable changes**. If you want to get in the habit of meditating, begin with just five minutes a day. Gradually increase the time as it becomes part of your routine.

- **Incorporating accountability partners** can also make a big difference. Share your goals with a friend or join a group with similar objectives. Having someone to check in with can keep you motivated and committed.

- **Reflect on your progress**. Take time to review what's working and what's not. Make adjustments as needed. You may find that meditating in the morning doesn't work for you, but doing it before bed does. Flexibility helps sustain long-term habits.

- Try **habit-stacking**, which builds new habits by linking them with established routines. Attach a new behavior to an existing routine (like brushing your teeth) to make remembering and adopting the new habit easier. This technique, popularized by James Clear in "Atomic Habits," helps make new behaviors more automatic.

Consider the story of Robin, who wanted to build a regular exercise routine. She started with short daily walks and gradually added more activities like yoga and strength training. Robin used a habit-tracking app to monitor her progress and shared her goals with a friend. Over time, exercise became a natural part of her day, and she noticed a significant improvement in her mental clarity and mood.

Then there's Neeraj, who struggled with poor diet and sleep habits. He decided to make small, incremental changes. Neeraj started by improving his breakfast, opting for nutritious oatmeal instead of sugary cereal. He also set a consistent bedtime, aiming to get at least seven hours of sleep each night. Neeraj used a journal to track his eating and sleeping patterns, reflecting on his progress weekly. These small changes added up, leading to better overall health and reduced overthinking.

Building long-term healthy habits is about making and sticking with small, sustainable changes. The key is consistency and reflection, whether starting a new exercise routine, improving your diet, or setting a consistent sleep schedule.

By understanding the habit loop, setting goals, and using habit-tracking tools, you can create habits that support your mental and physical well-being. And remember, it's okay to start small and adjust along the way. The important thing is to keep moving forward, one step at a time.

CHAPTER 10

COMMIT TO LONG-TERM CHANGE

Imagine you're a caterpillar, staring at another caterpillar as it disappears into a chrysalis, then emerges as a beautiful butterfly. The transformation looks daunting, maybe even impossible. You're mature and ready, but you're overthinking whether this might be too much.

Now, picture this metamorphosis as your long-term goal, whatever it might be. It seems overwhelming, but breaking it down into small, manageable steps makes it achievable. That's what we're tackling here: how to set short-term and long-term goals to guide you through that transformation, one step at a time.

Set Short-Term and Long-Term Goals

Setting goals is like giving your life a selected route on a GPS. Without them, you're just wandering aimlessly, hoping to end up somewhere good. Goals provide direction and purpose. They transform vague aspirations into tangible targets.

Think of goals as the locations you enter into your GPS. They chart your path and keep you motivated, confident, and committed. When you have a clear destination, you don't overthink the route; every step you take feels meaningful. Plus, goals allow you to track your progress and celebrate milestones, which is crucial for maintaining momentum.

SMART Goals

Let's discuss the **SMART goals** framework, a tried-and-true method for setting effective goals. **SMART** stands for **Specific, Measurable, Achievable, Relevant,** and **Time-bound** goals.

- First, define **specific** goals by answering questions like:
    - What exactly do I want to achieve?
    - Who's involved?
    - What resources do I need?
- Next, make your goals **measurable**. Instead of saying, "I want to be healthier," say, "I want to lose 10 pounds in three months." This specificity helps you track progress and know when you've succeeded.
- Ensure your goals are **achievable**. While it's great to aim high, setting impossible goals sets you up for failure.
- Verify that each goal is **relevant** by aligning it with your long-term aspirations and values. If it doesn't align, you will struggle to commit to it.

- To make a goal **time-bound**, set a deadline to keep you on track and define when you will assess your progress.

Creating a personal growth plan is like designing a blueprint for your future.

- Start by setting both short-term goals and long-term goals or aspirations. Short-term goals are the stepping stones to your long-term aspirations.

- Break your goals down into specific, actionable steps. For example, if your long-term goal is to run a marathon, a short-term goal might be to run three miles without stopping.

- Assign realistic deadlines and milestones to keep yourself accountable.

- Identify resources you'll need, like books, courses, and support networks.

When developing your plan, reflect on your current strengths and areas for improvement. Prioritize goals based on what truly matters to you. Perhaps career growth is your top priority, or improving your health takes precedence.

Create a vision board or mindmap like the one shown here to visualize your goals and the necessary steps. This visual representation can be a powerful motivator.

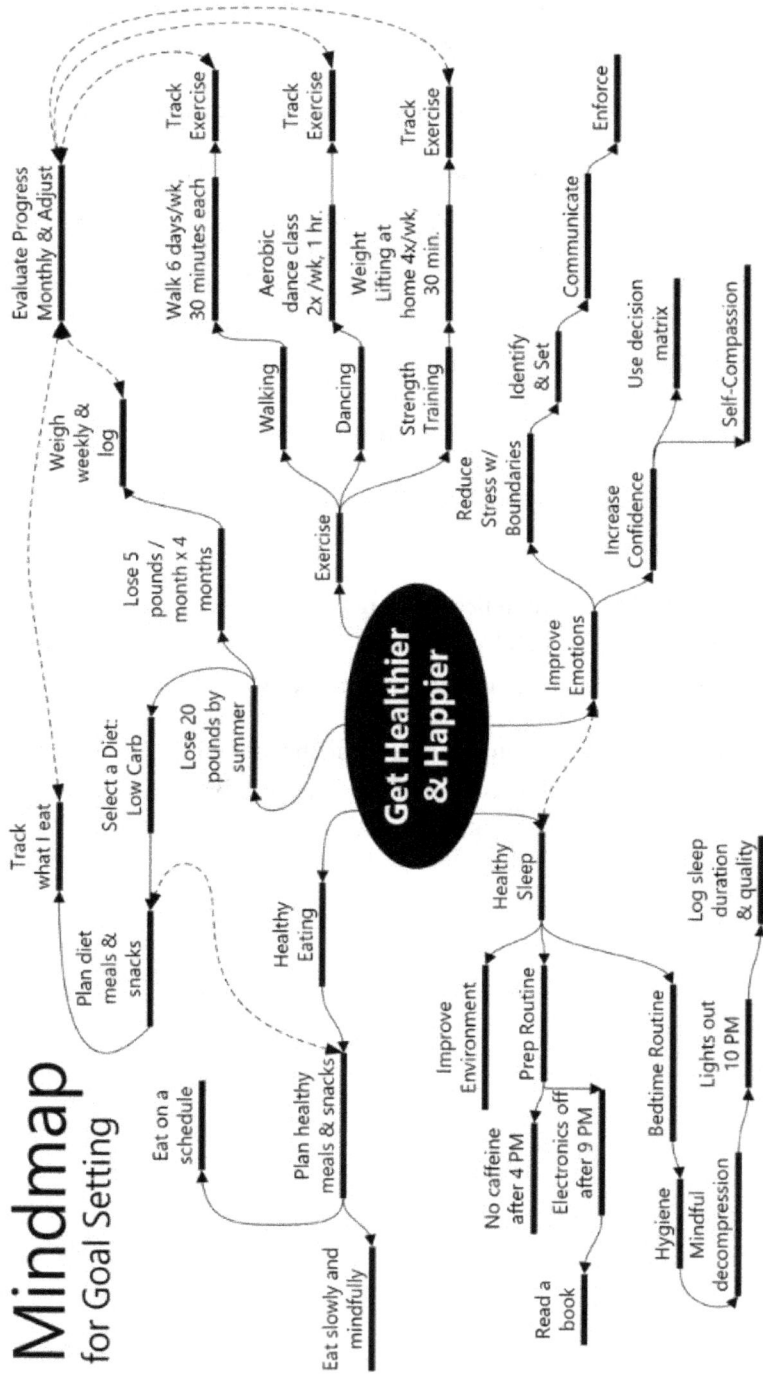

Use practical tools and templates to help you get started.

- **Goal-setting worksheets** can guide you through defining and refining your goals.

- Progress **tracking templates** help you monitor your journey and adjust as needed.

- The sample **SMART Goals worksheet** shown on the next page in the book includes goal setting, progress tracking, and adjusting.

  - Write your long-term aspirations at the top, then list up to four goals on the rows.

  - For each goal, fill in the five columns to identify what makes the goal specific, measurable, achievable, relevant, and time-bound.

  - Save the last column for later, when you will fill in your evaluation of your progress on each goal and revisions needed going forward.

  - Copy this worksheet or design your own.

SMART Goals Planner©

OVERTHINKING - The Silent Saboteur©
by Delia Sikes

Long Term Aspirations							Planned for Period:
							Month(s) & Year
							Planned Date
							Evaluation Date

Current Goal	S — Specific: What specifically am I trying to achieve?	M — Measurable: How will I measure success?	A — Achievable: What steps will I take to achieve this goal?	R — Relevant: Is this relevant to my long-term aspirations at this time?	T — Time-Bound: By when will I achieve this goal?	Evaluating Progress and Next-Time Steps: Making progress? Achieved? Revise for next time? Continue as-is?
1						
2						
3						
4						

- **Reflective journaling** (writing what you feel) can keep you focused and provide insights into your progress.

Consider the story of Megan, who set a fitness goal using the SMART framework. She wanted to lose 20 pounds in six months. At first, she wasted a lot of time overthinking the easiest way to lose weight while waiting for inspiration to strike. Then, she found motivation and stayed on track when she broke down this 20-pound goal into short-term goals of losing five pounds per month. With a clear plan, she celebrated each milestone and stayed focused on her ultimate goal.

Then there's Zach, an investment professional who aimed to advance his career. He set a long-term goal to become a division director within five years. He knew there would be competition for such a position, and simple tenure wouldn't get him there. He set short-term goals like completing leadership training and taking on challenging projects, which elevated him in the eyes of the executive leadership team, and he steadily climbed the corporate ladder.

Exercises

10A. Turn aspirations into SMART goals.

- Write down your long-term aspirations.
- Create SMART goals for one or more aspirations.

10B. Draw a mindmap or vision board to visualize your goals and brainstorm the steps. This can be done with a digital tool, a whiteboard and markers, or a pencil and paper.

- Put your aspiration in the center and your SMART goals around it.
- Add branches to the goals and fill in the steps to reach your SMART goals.

Be Consistent and Patient

Imagine you've decided to learn the guitar. You're all set with your shiny new instrument, a book of chord fingering, a pile of ambitious sheet music, and the excitement of becoming the next Jimi Hendrix. But as the days pass, the initial thrill fades, replaced by frustration when your fingers refuse to cooperate. This can be incredibly frustrating for talented people who aren't used to struggling. Here's where consistency becomes your best friend.

Building new skills and habits through repetition is vital to long-term success. Each time you pick up that guitar, even for just ten minutes, you're reinforcing positive behaviors. Over time, these small efforts accumulate, leading to gradual improvement. **Consistency** transforms those frustrating practice sessions into the sweet tunes of progress.

To stay **consistent,** create daily routines and schedules.

- Set aside specific times for your activities, whether practicing guitar, exercising, or working on a personal project.

- Use reminders and alarms to keep you on track. A sticky note on your fridge or a buzzing notification on your phone could work well.

- Track your progress with journals or apps so you don't overthink your level of effort. There's something incredibly satisfying about seeing your small steps add up over time.

- Whether you use a fitness app to log your runs or a journal to note your daily practice sessions, these tools can keep you motivated and accountable.

In addition to consistency, you need **patience** to steady your boat during the storm. It's the antidote to overthinking.

- Patience is understanding that change doesn't happen overnight.

- Patience is managing your expectations and avoiding the trap of overthinking and frustration when progress seems slow.

- Celebrating small victories helps maintain motivation so that being patient doesn't become monotonous. You may have mastered a new chord or run an extra mile. These moments are worth acknowledging. They're the tollgates along the road to your bigger goals.

- Practicing mindfulness and self-compassion can also cultivate patience. When you hit a roadblock, instead of overthinking it, take a deep breath and remind yourself that setbacks are part of the process.

- Breaking large goals into smaller, manageable steps can make them feel less daunting. For example, instead of tackling all the guitar chords at once, concentrate on the C-major and G-major chords.

- Seeking inspiration from role models and mentors can provide a motivational boost. They've been where you are and can offer valuable insights into the learning curve so you don't overthink it.

- Reflecting on your progress and adjusting your strategies as needed ensures you stay on course. If something isn't working, tweak it. Flexibility is key to maintaining momentum and achieving long-term success.

Exercises

10C. Plan for consistency and patience with repeating steps and milestones.

- Identify when and where you will make time for the repeating steps to reach your goals (e.g. exercising, practicing.)

- Decide where and how to track those repeating activities (e.g., an app, a spreadsheet, a calendar, or a journal.)

- Break your goals into interim milestones to celebrate along the journey.

- Note these details on your mindmap or vision board

Build a Support System for Ongoing Success

Imagine you're running that marathon we talked about earlier. Now, picture doing it alone versus having a group of friends cheering you on, handing you water, and helping you navigate tricky paths. That's the power of a support system.

A good support network is vital for sustaining long-term change because it provides accountability and encouragement. It's like having a built-in cheering squad that keeps you motivated and resilient. When you're feeling down or overthinking your plans, these people remind you why you started, reassure you, and push you to keep going. They offer diverse perspectives and advice, which can be invaluable when you're stuck or need clarification on your next steps.

Identifying potential support system members starts with looking around at the people already in your life.

- Friends and family members are often your first line of support. They know you well and can provide the emotional backing you need.

- Mentors and coaches are another excellent resource. They bring experience and wisdom, offering guidance and insight you might have yet to consider.

- Support groups and online communities can also be incredibly helpful. These groups are filled with people facing similar challenges and offer a sense of camaraderie and shared experience.

Building and maintaining a support system requires effort but is well worth it.

- Schedule regular check-ins and updates with your support network to keep everyone on the same page. These can be as simple as a weekly phone call or a monthly coffee date.

- Set up accountability partnerships to take it a step further. Find someone whose goals align with yours and agree to hold each other accountable. This could mean weekly progress reports or daily check-ins to motivate each other.

- Participate in group activities and discussions in person or online to foster a sense of community and shared purpose.

Take Roxanne, for example. She benefited immensely from having a mentor guide her through a career transition. Her mentor's advice on navigating office politics and developing leadership skills was invaluable.

Or consider Marty, who found a support group for people dealing with anxiety. The group provided emotional support and practical tips for managing stress, helping Marty trust his goals and achieve long-term change.

These testimonials highlight the transformative power of a robust support system, underscoring its importance in any journey toward personal growth and change.

Exercises

10D. Decide who you want to be your support network for achieving your goals and note them on your mindmap or vision board.

- Consider friends and family
- Consider mentors and coaches
- Consider support groups and online communities

Adopt Apps for Mindfulness and Stress Management

Imagine you're in the middle of a chaotic day, and your mind is racing. You're juggling work tasks, family responsibilities, and a never-ending to-do list. What if you could pull out your phone and find a moment of calm? The advantage of mindfulness and stress management apps is that they offer guided practices anytime, anywhere. These apps are designed to fit your busy schedule, providing various features tailored to your needs, from quick breathing exercises to longer meditation sessions. Whether a beginner or a seasoned meditator, these apps seamlessly integrate with your everyday technology to offer accessible support.

Apps for Mindfulness

- One of the top mindfulness apps is **Headspace**. It's known for its user-friendly interface and extensive library of guided meditations. Headspace covers everything from beginner courses to advanced practices, plus it offers sleep aids like bedtime stories and calming sounds.

- **Calm** is another fantastic option, especially if you want more flexibility. It provides a mix of guided and unguided meditations, focusing on relaxation and mindfulness. Calm's sleep stories are popular for helping users wind down at the end of the day.

- **Insight Timer** stands out with its community features and a vast collection of free guided meditations. It's perfect for those who enjoy connecting with others on their mindfulness journey.

- **Simple Habit** is great for busy people. It offers short, targeted sessions that fit even the most hectic schedules.

APPS FOR STRESS MANAGEMENT

- Regarding stress management, apps like **Breathe2Relax** offer guided breathing exercises and stress tracking. It's like having a personal coach in your pocket, guiding you through techniques to calm your mind and body.

- **Pacifica** combines cognitive behavioral tools with mood tracking to help you manage anxiety and stress.

- **Happify** uses science-based activities and games to boost your mood and reduce stress.

- **MyLife Meditation** offers personalized mindfulness recommendations based on mood check-ins, making it easy to find the right practice for your feelings.

GETTING STARTED

- Choosing the right app can feel overwhelming. Start with free trials to help you explore each one's features. Look for apps that resonate with you, whether it's the style of guided meditations or the types of activities offered.

- After selecting one, set reminders for regular practice to build a consistent routine.

- Combining app use with other mindfulness techniques, like journaling or breathing exercises, can enhance your experience.

- Track your progress within the app to see how far you've come and stay motivated.

EXERCISES

10E. Mindfulness and Stress Management Apps – decide if they can meet your needs.

- If your goals include focusing on mindfulness, take note of these app names to consider along with others.

    - Headspace

    - Calm

    - Insight Timer

    - Simple Habits

- If your goals include focusing on Stress Management, take note of these app names to consider along with others.

    - Breathe2Relax

    - Happify

    - The Tapping Solution

    - Unplug Meditation

Incorporating these apps into your daily routine can make a significant difference in managing stress and finding moments of calm amidst the chaos. They offer a convenient and effective way to support your mental well-being, helping you stay grounded and focused.

Engage with an Online Support Community

Imagine sitting at home, overthinking and overwhelmed by a whirlwind of thoughts. It's late, and you can't call a friend because you don't want to wake them. This is where an online support community can be advantageous.

Benefits

- Connecting with others who understand your struggles can provide emotional support and encouragement when needed.

- Sharing tips and strategies with people in the same boat can help you find new ways to manage overthinking.

- Plus, knowing you're not alone can significantly reduce feelings of isolation, making the journey to better mental health less daunting.

- These communities also offer opportunities for learning and growth as members share their experiences and insights.

Finding an Online Support Community

Finding and joining an online support community is easier than you think. Start by searching for relevant forums and social media groups.

- Platforms like **Reddit** and **Facebook** have numerous mindfulness and mental health communities where you can find like-minded individuals.

- Participating in app-based communities, like those on **Insight Timer**, can be beneficial. These platforms often host groups centered around specific topics or practices, making it easy to find a niche that fits your needs.

- Explore specialized forums like **HealthUnlocked.com** or **7Cups.com**, which can provide additional resources and support tailored to your concerns.

Participating

Once you've found an online community, active participation can maximize the benefits.

- Begin by introducing yourself and sharing a bit about your experiences. This will help others get to know you and open the door for meaningful connections.

- Don't hesitate to ask questions and seek advice; these communities are filled with people eager to help.

- Offering support and encouragement to others can be incredibly rewarding and fosters a sense of camaraderie.

- Participate in discussions and group activities to stay engaged and benefit from the group's collective wisdom.

Creating a Support Network

Creating a personal support network can also be a powerful way to sustain long-term change.

- Start by organizing virtual meetups or support groups with friends, family, or colleagues who share similar goals.

- Regularly share resources and progress updates to keep everyone motivated and accountable.

- Setting collective goals and accountability measures ensures that everyone stays on track.

- Celebrating milestones and achievements together can make the journey more enjoyable and rewarding.

- Whether it's a virtual high-five or a group video call to celebrate a success, these moments of shared joy can strengthen your support network and motivate you.

Exercises

10F. Support Communities: Decide if they can meet your needs.

- If a support community can help you meet your goals, take note of these options to consider along with others.
  - Redditt Communities
  - Facebook Communities
  - Insight Timer app
  - Health Unlocked
  - 7 Cups (online and an app)
  - Start a new community

In an online support community, you're not just another user but part of a network where everyone's experiences and insights can make a difference. Being active and engaged helps you get the most out of these communities, turning them into a vital part of your strategy for overcoming overthinking. So, take that step to connect and engage—you might be surprised how much it can help.

Use Digital Tools to Track Progress and Stay Motivated

Imagine you're on a mission to improve your mental health and personal growth, but keeping track of your progress feels like herding cats. This is where digital tools come in handy. They offer real-time data collection and analysis, allowing you to see your progress clearly and visually. Think of it as your dashboard, showing how far you've come and where you need to go. These tools are customizable to fit your unique needs, whether it's tracking moods, habits, or milestones. Plus, they integrate seamlessly with other wellness practices to simplify keeping everything in one place.

Journaling Apps

Let's dive into some specific digital tools that can help you monitor your journey.

- **Moodlight** is an app for tracking your mood and mental health. It offers assessments that can help you understand your emotional patterns and triggers.

- **Clarity: CBT Self Help Journal** includes cognitive behavioral therapy for managing stress, anxiety, and low moods.

- Two apps, **Daylio** and **How We Feel,** combine a journal and mood tracker, giving you visual statistics for your emotional highs and lows.

- **Habit-Bull** is perfect for building and maintaining new habits, offering a straightforward way to track your daily routines.

- **Reflectly** uses AI to guide you through personal reflection and growth, making journaling like a conversation with a supportive friend.

Setting up these tools is a breeze.

- Start by creating your profile and setting your preferences.

- Customize tracking parameters and goals to align with your objectives.

- Input data regularly to keep your records up to date, and review your progress often to spot trends and areas for improvement.

- Use reminders and notifications to stay consistent. For example, set a daily reminder to log your mood in **Daylio** or check off your **Habit-Bull** habits.

Using Digital Tools to Stay Motivated

Staying motivated can be a challenge, but digital tools make it easier.

- Celebrate small wins and milestones to keep your spirits high. These tools often have built-in features for marking achievements, giving you a dopamine boost each time you hit a target.

- Reviewing your progress helps identify patterns and areas that need tweaking. It's like having a personal coach in your pocket, constantly nudging you to do better.

- Set new goals based on your collected data to keep moving forward.

- Participating in app-based challenges and community events can also add a fun, competitive element to your journey, keeping you engaged and motivated.

Exercises

10G. Journaling Apps: Decide if they can meet your needs.

- If your goals can benefit from digital journaling, take note of these app names to consider along with others.

    - Moodlight
    - Clarity
    - Daylio
    - How We Feel
    - Habit-Bull
    - Reflectly

Digital tools offer a convenient and effective way to stay on top of your mental health and personal growth. They transform the abstract concept of self-improvement into something tangible and trackable, making it easier to stay motivated and see real progress.

Real-Life Testimonials: Achieving Long-Term Success

Sharon's Story

Sharon, a healthcare management professional, was paralyzed by overthinking. She'd spend hours second-guessing every email and conversation, convinced she'd said the wrong thing. This kept her from taking on leadership roles and new projects.

Sharon decided to take control. She started small, implementing mindfulness practices and using progress-tracking tools. She set realistic goals and celebrated each milestone, no matter how small. Over time, her confidence grew. She began to trust her instincts and took on more responsibilities at work.

Her consistency and patience paid off, and she eventually earned a promotion. Sharon's story is a testament to how overcoming overthinking can lead to career success.

Martin's Story

Martin struggled with both mental health and relationships. He was often overwhelmed by anxiety, which affected his interactions with others.

Martin committed to improving his mental well-being through consistent effort. He used mindfulness apps and joined an online support community where he could share his experiences and learn from others. Tracking his progress, he celebrated small victories, like staying calm during stressful situations.

Over time, Martin noticed significant improvements in his mental clarity and reduced anxiety. His relationships improved as he became more present and engaged. Martin's journey shows the power of consistent effort in achieving better mental health and stronger relationships.

What made these transformations possible? Consistency and patience were crucial.

- Sharon and Martin applied new habits regularly, reinforcing positive behaviors until they became second nature.

- Each tracked their progress meticulously, celebrating milestones, which kept them motivated.

- Each also adapted to challenges, showing flexibility when things didn't go as planned. This adaptability allowed them to stay on course without becoming discouraged.

The outcomes they experienced were profound.

- Sharon's career flourished as she conquered overthinking. She gained mental clarity that allowed her to make decisions confidently. Her professional relationships improved as she became a reliable leader.

- The benefits were equally significant for Martin. He enjoyed better mental health, reduced anxiety, and more emotional stability. His personal relationships deepened as he learned to communicate more effectively and be present.

So, what can you take from these stories?

- Consistency and patience are your allies.

- Start small, track your progress, and celebrate your milestones.

- Adapt when faced with challenges and remain flexible.

- Remember, lasting change doesn't happen overnight. It's the cumulative effect of small, consistent efforts.

- As Sharon's and Martin's stories show, taming overthinking can lead to a more fulfilling life, both professionally and personally.

No matter how small, each step brings you closer to your goals. Whether it's enhancing your career, improving your mental health, or building stronger relationships, the strategies you've learned here can guide you. Stay consistent, be patient, and remember to celebrate your progress. Your journey to lasting change is well within reach.

Conclusion

We are at the end of our journey together, but I want to share something that could make all the difference.

A Challenge for You

Do you recall that we reviewed the **Pareto Principle**, also called the 80/20 Rule? It suggests that 80% of your results come from 20% of your efforts, so focus on what's important.

Don't ignore what you've learned in this book. **Identify and implement the top 20% of its ideas that best align with your needs.** That's your high-impact reward; claim it.

- You're armed with tools to silence that relentless mind chatter.

- Recognize the triggers that launch your overthinking and use the tools to deactivate them.

- Use the best decision-making frameworks to break out of analysis paralysis.

- Break negative thought patterns with mindfulness, guided breathing, and visualization techniques. These aren't fluffy concepts; they're proven methods for calming your mind and shifting focus.

- Build your self-confidence with self-compassion, positive affirmations, and patience.

- Improve your sleep quality with the right environment and bedtime rituals.

- Overcome self-sabotage by tackling procrastination, setting realistic goals, and managing time effectively.

- Improve personal relationships with clear communication and healthy boundaries. Practice active listening and resolve conflicts without letting overthinking intervene.

Mental clarity, confident decisions, better relationships, and long-term well-being are within your reach. Take immediate action, even if it's just a small step.

Gradually build on your progress and remember to track your journey and celebrate your milestones.

Thank you for your time and commitment to reading ***Overthinking – The Silent Saboteur***.

Conquering overthinking is a journey that requires ongoing effort and commitment, and you're well on your way.

Warm regards,
Delia Sikes

Review Request

Your voice is powerful. Many people decide which books to read based on recommendations like yours. That's why I'm asking you to leave a review for **Overthinking—The Silent Saboteur**. It's a small, simple act that takes less than a minute but can profoundly impact someone's life.

Ready to help someone else silence their overthinking? It's easy! Just go to this book on Goodreads or on the website for the company from which you purchased the book, and leave your review with a rating, a video or photo, and your thoughts.

If this book has touched you, consider passing it on to someone who might benefit from it.

More Books by Delia Sikes

Please check out the companion book, ***Empathy Unlocked - Learning to Connect in a Disconnected World***, or the combination book, **Empathy and Overthinking –Navigating Your Inner and Interpersonal Worlds**.

Please also check out Delia's book, **I'm Not Toxic, You're Overreacting**.

REFERENCES

Overthinking: Definition, Causes, \u0026 How to Stop
https://www.berkeleywellbeing.com/overthinking.html

How to recognize and tame your cognitive distortions
https://www.health.harvard.edu/blog/how-to-recognize-and-tame-your-cognitive-distortions-202205042738

Executive control and decision-making in the prefrontal ...
https://www.sciencedirect.com/science/article/pii/S2352154614000278

Stress Symptoms: Physical Effects of Stress on the Body
https://www.webmd.com/balance/stress-management/stress-symptoms-effects_of-stress-on-the-body

Recognizing overthinking and how to stop: DBT Emotion ...
https://www.kindmindpsych.com/recognizing-overthinking-and-how-to-stop-dbt-emotion-regulation-skills/

The CBT Technique That's Overlooked, Undervalued, And ...
https://www.psychologytools.com/articles/the-cbt-technique-thats-overlooked-undervalued-and-essential-why-is-self-monitoring-so-important/

How to Stop Overthinking Your Relationship
https://greatergood.berkeley.edu/article/item/how_to_stop_overthinking_your_relationship

The Cognitive Impact of Past Behavior: Influences on ...
https://www.ncbi.nlm.nih.gov/pmc/articles/PMC4807731/

The Eisenhower Matrix: How to prioritize your to-do list
https://asana.com/resources/eisenhower-matrix

DECIDE Decision-Making Model
https://winapps.umt.edu/winapps/media2/wilderness/toolboxes/documents/safety/DECIDE%20Decision-Making%20Model.pdf

How to Overcome Your Fear of Making Mistakes
https://hbr.org/2020/06/how-to-overcome-your-fear-of-making-mistakes

How to Stop Overthinking and Start Trusting Your Gut
https://hbr.org/2022/03/how-to-stop-overthinking-and-start-trusting-your-gut

Getting Started with Mindfulness
https://www.mindful.org/meditation/mindfulness-getting-started/

How Breath-Control Can Change Your Life: A Systematic ...
https://www.ncbi.nlm.nih.gov/pmc/articles/PMC6137615/

How to Use Visualization to Reduce Anxiety Symptoms
https://www.verywellmind.com/visualization-for-relaxation-2584112

Self-affirmation activates brain systems associated with ...
https://www.ncbi.nlm.nih.gov/pmc/articles/PMC4814782/

How To Silence Your Inner Critic: A Four-Step Approach
https://www.betterhelp.com/advice/self-esteem/how-to-silence-your-inner-critic/

The Benefits of Self-Compassion in Mental Health ...
https://www.ncbi.nlm.nih.gov/pmc/articles/PMC9482966/

12 Ways to Have More Confident Body Language
https://www.verywellmind.com/ten-ways-to-have-more-confident-body-language-3024855

Emotional regulation: Skills, exercises, and strategies
https://www.betterup.com/blog/emotional-regulation-skills

Stressed to the max? Deep sleep can rewire the anxious ...
https://news.berkeley.edu/2019/11/04/deep-sleep-can-rewire-the-anxious-brain/

12 Tips for Better Sleep Hygiene
https://www.healthline.com/health/sleep-hygiene

Blue light has a dark side - Harvard Health
https://www.health.harvard.edu/staying-healthy/blue-light-has-a-dark-side#:~:text=Harvard%20researchers%20and%20their%20colleagues,as%20much%20(3%20hours%20vs.

Four of the Best Sleep Meditation Apps, According to Experts
https://www.sleep.com/sleep-tech/four-of-the-best-sleep-meditation-apps

Overcoming Self-Sabotage in the Workplace
https://www.innovativehumancapital.com/article/overcoming-self-sabotage-in-the-workplace

How To Overcome Procrastination
https://www.mindtools.com/a5plzk8/how-to-stop-procrastinating

How This Entrepreneur Finally Stopped the Cycle of Self- ...
https://www.entrepreneur.com/leadership/how-this-entrepreneur-finally-stopped-the-cycle-of/379095

The Importance of Communication in Relationships | Florida
https://iditsharoni.com/the-importance-of-communication-in-relationships-how-to-build-stronger-connections-with-your-partner/

7 Active Listening Techniques For Better Communication
https://www.verywellmind.com/what-is-active-listening-3024343

How to Set Boundaries in Your Relationships
https://psychcentral.com/relationships/why-healthy-relationships-always-have-boundaries

Strategies for Conflict Resolution
https://www.mandtsystem.com/2019/04/15/strategies-for-conflict-resolution/

Nutritional psychiatry: Your brain on food
https://www.health.harvard.edu/blog/nutritional-psychiatry-your-brain-on-food-201511168626

11 Best Foods to Boost Your Brain and Memory
https://www.healthline.com/nutrition/11-brain-foods

The Mental Health Benefits of Exercise
https://www.helpguide.org/wellness/fitness/the-mental-health-benefits-of-exercise

A Holistic Approach to Mental Health
https://onlinedegrees.nku.edu/programs/healthcare/msn/pmhnp/holistic-approach-to-mental-health/

Goal Setting Basics: Long-Term And Short-Term Goals For ...
https://www.speexx.com/speexx-blog/goal-setting-basics-long-term-and-short-term-goals-for-success/

How to write SMART goals (with examples)
https://www.atlassian.com/blog/productivity/how-to-write-smart-goals

Personal Development Plan Templates for Success
https://www.briantracy.com/blog/personal-success/personal-development-plan/

The 4 Best Meditation Apps of 2024 | Reviews by Wirecutter
https://www.nytimes.com/wirecutter/reviews/best-meditation-apps/

Hoopoe
Quotes https://www.hoopoequotes.com/occasions/good-night-messages/item/35011-the-best-bridge-between-despair-and-hope-is-a-good-night-s-sleep-hope-you-have-a-restful-night

Chat GPT.(2024). Chat GPT GPT-4 [Software]. Open AI.
https://openai.com/chatgpt

www.ingramcontent.com/pod-product-compliance
Lightning Source LLC
Chambersburg PA
CBHW060500030426
42337CB00015B/1659